EARLY PRAISE FOR *LIVING THE LIFE OF LIGHT*

"While the Christian New Testament Bible instructs Christians to become more like Jesus the Christ, a body of Christian knowledge revealing the mystical process whereby human consciousness transforms to divine consciousness is lacking in mainstream Christianity. The book *Living the Life of Light* provides such wisdom, and with scholastic rigor relates the "Odes of Solomon" to the New Testament and early Christian history in various ways. In so doing it documents the Odes' Christian heritage and links transformational spiritual practices to the earliest Christian communities. It reveals the path of transformation that was available to the early Christians and was subsequently lost until recent times. The poet-author of the Odes describes his timeless spiritual experiences such that anyone familiar with these experiences can recognize them, but since few are familiar with these experiences, someone who is familiar must decode the Odes to bring out their wisdom for the many to benefit.

"Fortunately, the author of *Living the Life of Light* is familiar with these experiences, and he has also learned the languages that were needed to decipher the Odes: Sahidic Coptic (the language of the Nag Hammadi Library) and Syriac (the written form of the Aramaic dialect spoken across the Middle East in the first and second centuries). Combining powerful scholastic skills with his spiritual experience, he has broken new ground on the inner meaning of the Odes that should be of value to truth seekers from any religion."

— DAVID MITCHELL, President, Divine Mission

"Robert Petrovich has worked very hard on this book with its translations, including mastering some four languages to do so. His translations of the Odes are not only precise but also as

poetic as he could possibly render them in Modern English. As he presents them, he demonstrates that the Odes of Solomon in their numbered sequence tell a dramatic tale of Ascent into Light and personal spiritual transformation. In his view, the pure form of the teaching we know as early Christianity that he considers the Odes to exemplify was both the fulfillment of the "Messianic Expectations" of so-called "Essene Doctrine" we supposedly know from the Dead Sea Scrolls, but also the mystic form of "Jewish Christian," "Ebionite" Teaching, which was lost when Pauline and Nicene Doctrines changed this aboriginal "Messianism" into the present form we now know as "Christianity" in the Fourth Century – the same period of time that the Odes of Solomon and their teaching of spiritual transformation nearly disappeared from the face of the Earth. "

—Robert Eisenman, author of *James the Brother of Jesus* and *The New Testament Code*

"The Odes of Solomon is one of the best reflections of piety and devotion to Christ in early Jewish Christianity, and for a period of at least three centuries they were reckoned as Scripture by some early churches and their leaders. Although considerable scholarship has been expended on the translation and interpretation of these spiritual songs in recent years, the Odes are still largely unknown to most laypersons in churches today. Robert Petrovich has produced a carefully prepared translation with some commentary on the Odes and on their history that will aid considerably in a renewed interest in the Odes. Those of us who have examined their function and importance for understanding the piety and spiritual development of early Christianity are grateful to have this new and informed translation with important notes on the history and function of the Odes' reception up through the fourth century. I am pleased to recommend this work without reservation not only for church laity, but also for biblical scholars who are less familiar with the Odes and their history."

—Lee Martin McDonald, Acadia Divinity College
and author of *The First Known Christian Songbook*

"An excellent work I highly recommend."

—Willis Barnstone, Distinguished Professor of Comparative Literature, Indiana University, editor of *The Gnostic Bible* and author of *Poets of the Bible From Solomon's Song of Songs to John of Revelation*

"Gnosis has become a popular spiritual tech for modern esoterica, fueled by the interest in Gnosticism and lost gospels. Many suspect it originated before the rise of the Gnostics in early Christian times. The Odes of Solomon makes a strong case for this. Robert Petrovich takes us on a spanning journey of this poetic, inspirational, and unique text in his book, granting the reader not only the secrets of Gnosis but a view of a sophisticated, spiritual community trying to understand the mysteries of existence. Highly recommended for both seekers and aficionados of historical apocrypha!"

—Miguel Connor, host of Aeon Byte Gnostic Radio and author of *Gnostic Voices* and *Other Gnostic Voices*

Living the Life of Light
A Drama of Ascension

Living the Life of Light
A Drama of Ascension

~

A Translation of The Odes of Solomon
from the Syriac and Commentary

BY ROBERT PETROVICH

JAMILIAN UNIVERSITY PRESS

JAMILIAN UNIVERSITY PRESS

Copyright © 2018 by Robert Petrovich. All rights reserved. Except for brief quotations in critical articles or reviews, no part of this book may be reproduced without prior written permission from the publisher.

All cross images are in public domain except for the Second Advent Solar Cross, which is a registered trademark of the International Community of Christ and Cosolargy® International and is used with permission.

First Edition Paperback
ISBN 978-1-949360-00-4

Front Cover Image © wittayawic | istock.com

10 9 8 7 6 5 4 3 2 1

My spiritual colleagues helped with these translations over the two years I have worked on them, and I want especially to thank Robert Anderson and my wife, Francine Petrovich.

I am also grateful for the spiritual and liturgical training I received over the past thirty some years from The Most Right Reverend Gene Savoy in the Sacred College of the Jamilian University of the Ordained.

Contents

~

XIII | Preface

XIX | Introduction

3 | Odes of Solomon: The Messianic Drama

225 | Remarks On The Life and Times
of The Odes of Solomon as Conclusion

TWO AFTERWORDS

243 | Three Poets on Translating Poetry
257 | The Project of Translating the Odes of Solomon

Preface

In the Odes of Solomon there is no grief and no complaint — only joy and praise. There is loss and there is danger, but these are always offset by knowledge and faith. The joy is ecstatic, and the ecstasy is the ecstasy of divine love. The praise is the praise of All and the Father of All — the Lord God. Not because God requires or needs praise but because all Life is the glory of God. The Syriac word for *praise* is the same as the word for *glory*, and this is how praise makes clear the glory of God. And the acquisition of spiritual glory — the Light of the poet and the Light of the holy ones whom he speaks of and speaks to — is itself a form of praise of God. The Odes depict the Life which this Light engenders, and this Life is a drama that is lived and relived by every Child of Light in every age. Simply put, it is the Life of Light.

The collection of Odes was perhaps not intended by the author to be a monumental work — but it is. Whether the Odes were written by one author or many, whether they were arranged in sequence by the author or by someone else, they embody one spirit and one thought — and we do not always find thought in poems. Every poet contributes feeling. Most poets contribute perception. More rarely, a poet contributes perception and also thinks. The poet of the Odes is certainly one of these. And he is obviously a spiritual adept, full of spiritual knowledge. The poet, in fact, tells us as much.

Thinking can bring new force into a poem. But there is also the risk that a reader may find in a poem an idea which the reader believes to be untrue and so reject the whole poem. That is one of the difficulties of bringing the Odes into the twenty-first century: the doctrines they represent are not familiar to those who call themselves Christian. They do not correspond to Roman doctrines, either Eastern or Western, nor the doctrines of any modern Reformed church, nor the doctrines of any present Eastern Church. Yet the doctrines of the Odes stand as the predecessor and the progenitor of them all.

Another difficulty is the ancient imagery, which is at times unusual to us. References are made in the Odes to images of God and spirit, including the Dark spirit, that in our time appear exotic. For their time, these cultural references and the doctrines they represent may have been pointedly clear to one who was raised or trained in their specific spiritual tradition. Even the images that are drawn from nature, which may seem familiar, pose difficulties, because they are actually metaphors that extend far beyond nature into supranatural, or nonphysical, experience. Yet it is only in our own time that the core meaning of the Odes of Solomon may again be received with understanding.

The doctrines of the Odes are ancient, their origins beyond time. One of the last places on Earth these doctrines were practiced communally in a spiritual society was in ancient Syria-Palestine. The Essenes were a remnant of True Israel there that continued to follow the True Way. In the ritual of their daily liturgy they revered the spiritual power carried in the light of the Sun. But their doctrines of the Way had grown rigid and severe over the centuries, and they awaited their promised Messiah and Teacher to interpret the times for them and to fulfill the scriptures and amend them. And when the Messiah came, there were many among them who recognized the coming of renewed spiritual power and the teachers of this power. It was these teachers and their disciples who grew into the messianic Community that produced the Odes. And this Community continued to use the same spiritual idiom as those more ancient holy ones, the Essenes and the pious predecessors of the Essenes. And this Community continued to follow the ancient doctrines — modified and amended, of course, by the fact that the long-awaited Messiah figure had arrived, had been active in their midst, and had taught them by interpreting and fulfilling scripture.

Sometime about one hundred years before the Common Era, a Prophet Messiah — whose name has been lost and who is known to us from ancient writings only as "the Star" (and who perhaps was the author of the Book of Hymns in the Dead Sea scriptures) — had roused this remnant and pointed them again toward the living Way. Generations later, a Priest Messiah called them out and a Lay Messiah gathered and led them. The personal Messiah of that age, the expected Lay Messiah, was known by various titles. The "Son of Man" was one of them. He was expected to come from either the house of David or the house of Aaron, depending upon one's belief tradition. In the Gospel of Matthew, Jesus refers to the priest John (known to Christians in our times as either John the Baptist or John the Forerunner, depending upon one's belief tradition) as Elijah, who, according to prophecy, was to precede the personal Messiah; and in the same gospel, Jesus refers to himself as the Son of Man. The members of the messianic Community that followed John and Jesus were despised by those who upheld the conventions of the nation's popular religion. They held to the new Way and sought sanctuary, and they were pursued. Eventually, they were dispersed, and they and their Way were slowly extinguished.

The author of the Odes describes the experience of the Way as it was offered to him under the conditions of his age: in spiritual company with the personal Messiah, the resurrected "One Who Does Not Die." The process of redemption is the same now as it was then, and it is accomplished through the same stages of spiritual regeneration. These stages are implicit, or assumed, in the Odes. And for those who practice this Way, the images employed by the poet to depict his personal experience of spiritual transformation and regeneration are clear and recognizable because they are images of their own experience.

The Odes are not a lesson book, and so they do not lay out a step-by-step guide to this process. But, together, they are the personal expression of one who has experienced the process and celebrates it. The stages of personal spiritual growth are alluded to throughout the series, usually for the purpose of setting the context of each poem in a particular eternal moment. And so it is possible to see the stages of this process reflected in the images that the poet of the Odes has used to depict his own experience of them.

Despite the trauma of events that followed the arrival of the human Messiah, the Way that the Messiah taught and the purpose of the spiritual nation that he was to lead remain the same. In our time, the Way has been revealed again, renewed with new amendments for our age. The Dead Sea scriptures speak of this time at the end of the world, when a messianic kingdom would be established by direct intervention of God. So does the prophet Malachi (see Malachi 4:1–6). In our time there is to be no human Messiah that can be tormented and put down. In our time God has appeared through the Image that the human Messiah had revealed in his time — the Sun of Righteousness — and the image of the Cross that is God's Seal, called in the Odes "the Cross of Uprightness." Then as now, it is through the Light of God's Messianic Sun that we are to be redeemed.

It is my hope that in our own time the meaning of the Odes can again be received with understanding. To encourage this understanding is the intention of the new translation and commentary in this book.

–Robert Petrovich, 2017

Introduction

I took off Darkness
and clothed myself with Light;
*   and then I had limbs for my soul,*
in which there was no pain,
nor sickness, nor suffering.
   —21ˢᵀ Ode of Solomon

What the Odes of Solomon are about

THE EXPERIENCE OF SPIRITUAL TRANSFORMATION, the personal and individual reception of divine nourishment and spiritual rebirth, is the experience of the Living One who is identified in the Odes as the Messiah, the Anointed One. He is a kind of second Adam, a new Son of God. He is able to renew the Covenant with God in full force, and he is knowledgeable in the deceiving ways of demons. He is spiritually attuned to receive the Word of God, and he is able to provide from that Word a new Teaching of The Way for those who are receptive to receive it — those who are his spiritual kin, those who await the promised Messiah. The Messiah, this first new Living One—the first to experience personally the Second Coming of God—was, according to the New Testament tradition, held captive by the rulers of the world, hung on a tree, and put to death with an iron lance thrust into his side. In the Odes the name Jesus is never mentioned and the crucifixion is merely alluded to, and then only once. Not long after the historic event of the Crucifixion, a few generations perhaps, the Way of return to spiritual being was eclipsed again for another two millennia. Even so, it is clear that the poet who authored the Odes went through the same process of spiritual transformation that was undergone by the Anointed One and that the poet recounted his personal experience of the process in the Odes.

When and where the Odes of Solomon were written

The experiences expressed in the Odes take place outside of time, and they are too personal and interior to give any clear historical clue to the worldly origin of the Odes themselves. The few images that do seem to provide historical references may also, or may simply, be references to spiritual (nonphysical) archetypes. One thing can be said with certainty about the origin of the Odes: The historical period in which the Odes were written corresponds with a time when the first generations of the Living, those messianists following the Way of Spiritual Regeneration, still flourished in the lands in or around the Roman Empire, at a time when Gnosis still remained a worldwide spiritual Way and the intellectual teaching popularly known as Gnosticism had not yet developed. The author of the Odes, whoever he was and whatever his ethnicity, was a member of such a messianic Community, with Essenic roots, like the Communities that produced the Gospels of John, Philip, and Thomas. During the first centuries of our era, a scattering of such Communities existed in Egypt, in Mesopotamia, and in Roman Syria-Palestine, where the languages Greek, Aramaic-Syriac, and Latin were spoken, in that order of frequency.

Both the original composition of the Odes and a masterful translation of the Odes existed from early on, one in Syriac and one in Greek. Which was the original language of the Odes and which was the language of translation is not known for certain. During the first centuries of our era, great bilingual scholars like Bardaisan in Edessa were capable of composing the Odes in either language, and great bilingual churches like the one at Syrian Antioch were capable of singing them. There is general agreement that the Odes were originally composed in Syriac, but their spiritual idiom, no doubt the product of a long and developed oral tradition, had wide circulation among Greek-speaking peoples quite early as well. The evidence is plentiful: the metaphors and rhetorical figures employed in the Odes are paralleled in the Epistles of Ignatius of Antioch (c. 50–117), the Epistle of Barnabas (c. 70–131), the writings of Theophilus of Antioch (fl. 169–183), the Apology of Aristides (100s), the teachings of Montanus (fl. 135–177), and the various passages quoted as heretical by the famed Roman Christian polemicist Irenaeus (late 100s).

If the original *were* composed in Greek, it could only have been in western Syria, where the new community of covenanters under the disciples of Jesus first fled to seek refuge from political persecution, and at some time between the first Roman siege of Jerusalem in 70 and the final Jewish-Roman War of 132–136. After that time, Jews and Christians throughout the Roman Empire went their separate ways and all things Jewish were banned in Jerusalem except the celebration of Jewish defeat (a ban that remained in effect formally until the seventh century and informally until 1948). But the Odes indicate no such separation. If the Odes originated outside the influence of Rome, where Jewish and Christian traditions were not yet severed, the possible time frame for their composition lengthens. In the eastern kingdom of Edessa, for example, outside of direct Roman influence, the Odes were sung for nearly two centuries in the Mystery School of Bardaisan — until Rome and Roman ways invaded there in the third century and, in the fourth century, finally conquered, and the School moved farther east. In Mesopotamia, the Odes continued to be copied until at least the fifteenth century, the time when the latest manuscript copy that has come down to us was made. How long the Odes remained in use there as a common hymn book, and when they became merely an ancient relic, is a matter of conjecture.

Who wrote the Odes of Solomon

The Odist, whose name we do not know, was a mystic and a poetic genius. He apparently knew by heart the Davidic Psalms. His songs continue the Jewish psalter in the style of the Qumran Thanksgiving

Hymns and celebrate the same spiritual archetypes as their Essene authors. He, as another Living One, drinks the Living Water and receives a Body of Light. He takes part in the War of Light and Darkness and reveres the Sun of Spirit. He possesses Eternal Life and relegates those of Darkness not to the wrath of eternal punishment that is promised in the Hebrew Testament, but to extinction. The expression of his thought is akin to the Gospel of Truth of Valentinus, the Gospel of Thomas, the Gospel of Philip, and the Hymn of the Pearl, but not to the later, unforgiving Gnostic systems of the spiritually dispossessed. His verses move in free rhythms like the Qumran Hymns, full of joy and word play and internal rhyme. And he uses old words in new ways — another indication that the author is partaking of a new spiritual dispensation.

A major theme of the Odes is the attainment of God's rest — the repose, calm, or serenity that is a result of redemption in this new dispensation. In the biblical book 1 Chronicles (28:2), King David designates the Temple that is to be built, the Temple which God had deemed David unfit to build but which his son Solomon *would* build, as a "house of rest" for the ark of the covenant. Solomon's Temple is thought to have been oriented to the sun. What the exact orientation of the Temple was still remains a matter of conjecture. One thought is that the Golden gate to the city of Jerusalem, which was called the Gate of the Sun and faced East, was built so that the light of the rising Sun would fall upon it and enter the Holy of Holies at the time of the solstice; another that the Sun at its rising would fall upon the Holy of Holies over the ridge of the Mount of Olives on the equinoxes; another that the Sun would do so on a Sacred Calendar date like Passover. (All these propositions are based on, but cannot be verified by, literary data. Further archeological excavations on the Temple Mount might provide further evidence but have so far been prohibited by religious and cultural sensitivities.) In any case, the priests of Jerusalem later turned their backs on the Sun and faced the West when performing their rites. According to the doctrines of the Essenes, when the Messiah came, it would be to restore to Israel the ancient religion of Moses, a secret doctrine that had revolved around the light of the Sun.

After the destruction of Herod's Temple in 70 CE, the Temple crown was lost to the Hebrew people. With the New Covenant that was announced and exemplified by the Lord's Anointed One came fitting replacements for the main features of the old covenant. In the Odes of the New Covenant, the golden crown that was lost to the Jewish people after the destruction of the communal Jerusalem Temple was replaced by the "living crown" of the holy individual, and the communal "house of rest" was replaced by the "rest" achieved by the holy individual who is reconciled with God and redeemed. In the Old Covenant books, the king and poet Solomon is designated as the "man of rest" (1 Chronicles 22:9). In the New Covenant Odes, every redeemed individual, every Child of God, becomes a "man of rest." The allegory of Christ the Messiah as the true Solomon is discussed in an exegetical work of the fourth- or fifth-century, *Expositiones in Psalmes*, but it is not known whether this allegory is as old as the poems themselves or their title.

This discussion brings us to the naming of this collection of poems as the Odes of Solomon. In the Old Covenant books, Solomon is called the "beloved" of God. In the New Covenant Gospels, Jesus, the Messiah, is called the "beloved" of God. The designation of this collection of poems as the "Odes of Solomon" probably had much to do with these kinds of progressive changes in the Covenant with God, as well as the contemporary poetic tradition of attributing new writings to ancient and revered authors that are part of the same literary tradition. Writings attributed in this way to more ancient spiritual heroes are commonly called "pseudepigrapha," a term that literally means "falsely" attributed — that is, attributed to someone by whom they were not actually written. Writings like the Davidic Psalms and the Wisdom of Solomon, for instance, are usually considered pseudepigraphical. But there is nothing "false" about them. They were considered to embody the wisdom or spirit of the one to whom they were attributed and were dedicated to them. Other scriptural works are attributed to Solomon as well: two of the biblical Psalms, the canonical books Proverbs, Ecclesiastes, Song of Songs, and Wisdom, and another noncanonical collection of poems, The Psalms of Solomon. This other noncanonical collection of poems follow the Odes of Solomon in the only two manuscript collections of the Odes that have come down to us in Syriac.

The Psalms of Solomon

The Psalms of Solomon have come down to us in twenty Greek manuscripts and five Syriac manuscripts. All the Syriac manuscripts tend to resemble the earliest Greek version. It is generally supposed that the Psalms were originally composed in Hebrew, but no Hebrew manuscript has yet been found. The Greek translations appear to have been made in the first century CE. The events referred to in the Psalms suggest that the poems were written in the second half of the first century BCE. Psalms 2, 8, and 17 make references to a foreigner who came to Jerusalem and desecrated the temple and who died in Egypt, his body lying on a beach. These references fit the Roman general Pompey exactly. In 63 BCE Pompey came to Judea to invade Jerusalem in order to interfere in the struggles of the various political factions and was murdered in Egypt in 48 BCE.

The authors of the Psalms of Solomon make the claim that the pious can atone for sins without the temple rituals. For them, daily piety replaced the sacrificial system. They, like the Qumran community before them, believed that reverent prayer had replaced sacrifice in the Jerusalem temple. Through a creative reading of Leviticus, the author of the third Psalm reinterprets the Day of Atonement rituals, the animal sacrifices described in Leviticus 16, to espouse a new lifestyle and concludes that through prayer and fasting ordinary Jews can accomplish the ritual functions formerly granted to the temple priests — atonement or reconciliation with God. For the poets who produced this collection, atonement was more than mere elimination of individual sins. Atonement restored Jews to the original and proper relationship with God. In this respect also, the community of these poems resembles the Qumran sect, whose members viewed their settlements as substitute temples, worshiping and practicing apart from the temple establishment priests. For the community that used the Psalms of Solomon, their community and homes had become a substitute for the temple.

The focus on temple priests and temple rituals, and the solution to worship and sacrifice offered by the writers of the Psalms of Solomon, tells much about the community behind these poems. The focus on cultic matters reflects priestly concerns and implies that at least some of the authors were priests. The poets describe the expulsion from the temple as a past event, which suggests that these poems contain the recollections of the founding generation, whose members were likely opposition priests. The focus on the temple priests also tells us much about Jewish disputes over the operation of the sanctuary during the Hasmonean period (circa 140 – 63 BCE), some of which are also reflected in the Dead Sea Scrolls. They are disputes that continued throughout the time of the succeeding Herodian dynasty until the Roman destruction of the Jerusalem temple in 70 CE.

Each of the eighteen Psalms of Solomon abounds with allusions to scripture, as well as biblical phrases and vocabulary, and the authors of these poems apparently considered it essential to work within the framework of existing scripture rather than write something entirely new. The Psalms of Solomon as a collection of poems espouse a particular interpretation of Biblical scripture that is meant to adapt the sacred texts to a new historical situation: the loss of the Jerusalem temple. The authors of the Psalms of Solomon, like the authors of the Dead Sea Scrolls, emphasize the covenant of a restricted group within the state of Israel. This perspective represents an acute self-consciousness of being chosen not as a political nation but as a spiritual nation of individuals, a True Israel. For them, the temple priests by their actions had forsaken the covenant and therefore had lost not only their covenantal standing but also their status as priestly intermediaries. For the authors of the Psalms of Solomon, it is the covenant of *their* group within the state of Israel that is of paramount importance. The community of the Psalms of Solomon believed that they were both chastised and saved because of their lifestyle — reconciled with God without the temple.

The communal identity throughout the Psalms of Solomon and the reference to the "synagogues of the holy" in Psalm of Solomon 17 suggest that the collection of poems was originally written for a synagogue community and that they were produced for liturgical use. Headings like "with song" in Psalms of Solomon 15 and 17 and the superscription "hymn" in Psalms of Solomon 10, 14, and 16 imply a liturgical use and suggest that the collection was recited in liturgical services. Psalms 17 and 18 also contain a musical notation partway through: *diapsalma* in Greek and *selah* in Syriac. *Selah* is a common Hebrew musical direction that occurs at the end of some of the verses in the Davidic psalms. *Diapsalma*, the Greek equivalent, literally means "apart from the psalm." Both words are enigmatic but indicate a kind of interlude, an "interlude for strings," and may signify a change in melody or rhythm that emphasized the verse.

The Syriac translation of the Psalms of Solomon tells us even more about the original community behind these poems. Christians today do not include a separate collection of hymns in their Bibles. This was not always the case. In the two Syriac manuscripts of the forty-two Odes of Solomon that have come down to us, the Psalms of Solomon follow the Odes in continuous numbering. The first Psalm of Solomon in these manuscripts is numbered "forty-three." This continuous numbering suggests that the entire collection was used liturgically by Syriac-speaking Christians.

Texts, especially liturgical texts, are written to propagate doctrine, even if such propaganda is the endorsement or confirmation of a particular perspective that is already acknowledged by those who hear it. The Psalms of Solomon espouse a new interpretation of scripture that their authors believe fulfills the intent of the covenant. The recitation of these poems in worship would have served both to create a community and to teach a distinctive lifestyle apart from the temple cult. Those who later joined this group would have relived the experiences of the early members of the Psalms of Solomon's community through recitation of these poems. Through the genre of poetry, the teachings of these founders would have attracted new adherents who had not known the group's originators and who were not involved in the original crises that precipitated their expulsion and separation from the temple. It is among the later communities of these adherents that the Odes were produced.

The Odes of Solomon and the Psalms of Solomon

The placement of the Odes of Solomon before the Psalms of Solomon in the two manuscript collections that we have indicates the new and accepted prominence of the Odes in second-century communities of the holy. The Odes, and the teachings they represent, were a new outgrowth rooted in the old stock opposition doctrines of the Psalms of Solomon, an outgrowth that acknowledges and reveres their origin in the old opposition priesthood exemplified by the Qumran community and the widespread "many" which that community spoke for, and later by the messianic community that grew from it under the leadership of Jesus and James the Just and their successors.

    The two collections of poems express different attitudes, and this difference reflects the differences between the two communities. The Odes of Solomon take the doctrines espoused in the Psalms of Solomon a step further. The Psalms of Solomon hold wishes of ill-will to hypocrites and evil-doers and curse them. The Odes of Solomon do no such thing; they simply ask not to be harmed by such people. The Odes apply the doctrines of the Psalms of Solomon to the situation and conditions of a later century, and so supersede them for a new messianic collective that is doubly separated from the temple — in space and in time — and replace the solemn sense of loss and disorientation expressed in the Psalms happily with pure joy and affirmation for individuals of all collective communities of "the holy." And in the Odes it is the joyous putting on of the Light in purity that is the vehicle of salvation and reconciliation with God, not simply pious asceticism.

The place of the Odes of Solomon in early Christian liturgy

During the first few centuries after the founding of the messianic Community by Jesus, the liturgy of that Community was improvised from Jewish usage and adapted to the new situation that was created by the messianic teachings of Jesus. Musically, the worship of the first generations of Christians was centered on songs. Songs, in fact, may have constituted the major form of Christian music until the late third century.

In many Protestant churches, the congregation is reminded that their faith and sacred doctrines are neither rooted in nor come from a hymnbook but from scripture. In early antiquity, that distinction did not exist. In later antiquity, that distinction was never as sharp as it is today. According to a well-known passage in Ephesians, evidence of the fullness of the Spirit among the Pauline followers of the risen Christ is demonstrated in the lines: "sing psalms and hymns and spiritual songs [read "odes"] among yourselves, singing and making melody to the Lord in your hearts, giving thanks to God the Father at all times and for everything in the name of our Lord Jesus Christ" (Ephesians 5:19–20).

The elements of ritual practice that shaped the liturgical function of music in early church communities include improvised singing and primacy of the word over its musical setting. So says Tertullian (c. 155 – c. 240 CE) — "Anyone who can, either from holy scripture or from personal inspiration, is called into the middle [of the assembly] to sing to God" (*Apologeticus* 39:18). Eusebius (260/265 – 339/340 CE), too, speaks of "all the psalms and hymns written from the beginning by faithful brethren, which sing of Christ as the Word of God."

The earliest Christian hymns emerged in Greek-speaking areas, and one of those areas was Syria-Palestine. Early hymns took as their model the translations of the Davidic Psalms found in the Septuagint. The Odes of Solomon, one of the earliest forms of uniquely Christian ritual music, offer a whole book of such songs.

According to the Gospel of John, Jesus wished that his "joy" would be completed in his followers. If early Christianity was a call to freedom and a joyous relation with a loving Creator, then the Odes of Solomon were the perfect hymn book. The Odes are a lyrics-book of early Jewish-Christian praise songs about the recent advent of the Messiah that may have been taught to catechumens as part of their instruction. Some have speculated this to be the case. And the idea makes good sense. If the Odes were liturgical texts in early Christianity, their catechetical possibilities are reinforced by their parallels to the Apostolic and Qumran texts of the Two Ways. They represent a period or mind set when there was as yet no acknowledgment of a strict line drawn between Second Temple Judaism and Christianity as a Gentile-welcoming form of Second Temple Judaism.

It is clear from the New Testament and other early Christian writings that Christians, like their Jewish siblings, wrote many songs that reflected the essence of their faith and their adoration of God and that they sang these compositions in their liturgy. Without question, the early Christians inherited from their Jewish siblings many hymns and prayers that originated in temple worship and circulated in the synagogues. And the music of the Jewish Temple before its destruction must have been extraordinary. Only in the Temple were there hundreds of Levites chanting, harps, trumpets, drums, flutes, tambourines, and dancing young virgins. Among the Essene and other opposition groups, there would have been sectarian liturgies and chanting as well — but likely without such grand musical accompaniment.

In the first century after the destruction of the Temple in 70 CE, worship had to shift from the central temple to the thousands of synagogues in and outside Syria-Palestine. The large and skillful choir at the Temple of Jerusalem, supplied by a famous choir school attached to the Temple, would have been the model of the smaller synagogue choirs throughout ancient Israel.

And as a sect of Judaism, the early messianic Community would have inherited the styles but not the splendor of Jewish public worship. After attending synagogue services on the Sabbath, the early Christians repaired to the house of one of their members for the agape, or love feast. Synagogue cantors, too, no doubt attended the agape and brought with them a sophisticated music. The sophisticated poetry of the Odes, and the mention in the Odes of the kithara, a stringed instrument, to accompany this poetry, suggests this kind of sophisticated music.

In the period before biblical songs came to occupy an important place in the liturgy, Christians were already singing new poetical compositions. But the post-Nicene establishment church always looked upon such compositions as potentially dangerous, since they were often used as tools of propaganda to promote a variety of theologies unacceptable to the official Roman church. And so the Odes were probably not especially important for the development of the Western church. Their celebration of private piety directly to God certainly would have caused them to be unattractive for those who were defining the imperial Church.

Early songs like the Odes, settings of short nonbiblical poems, improvised in either text or tune and transmitted orally, aroused such fundamental concerns about the whole idea of hymns in post-Nicene church circles that songs were simply withdrawn from Roman liturgical use around 363–364 CE by order of the Council of Laodicea (canon 59). Given this state of affairs, little has survived from this first spring of messianic song. Of such songs, known as *idiotikoi* — that is, songs composed by private individuals — hardly any but the Odes of Solomon have survived. (The two best known hymns that survived in the Western post-Nicene rite are the *Gloria*, a morning hymn, and the *Phos hilarion*, a hymn that conveys the magic of a golden sunset, which is sung at vespers, or evening prayer, in the Byzantine rite.)

The Odes of Solomon as early communal songs

What little is known about the life and liturgical practices of the early Aramaic-speaking community is derived from the Odes of Solomon, the oldest and largest surviving collection of ancient sacred Christian hymns. The Odes are contemporaneous with some literature of the New Testament canon but exhibit an earlier phase of the Church when, like the Essenes, Community members went out early each morning before work, faced the rising Sun, and prayed together with arms outstretched, considering this outstretching the "sign of the cross." (See Odes 27 and 42.) That the Odes were originally used in Christian liturgical worship is further evidenced by the "Hallelujah" that appears at the end of each Ode. That the Odes of Solomon were circulated among a number of communities is shown by their discovery not only in Syriac but in Greek and Coptic as well.

Within the Christian communities of the time, the sacraments of Eucharist and Baptism were observed, but what these sacraments actually were was kept a closely guarded secret. Pliny the Younger, in a letter to the Roman emperor Trajan (ca. 113 CE) provided a glimpse into Christian practices of his time as he understood them:

> *It was their habit on a fixed day to assemble before daylight and sing by turns a hymn to Christ as a god; and then they bind themselves with an oath, not for any crime but not to commit theft or robbery or*

adultery, not to break their word, and not to deny a deposit when demanded. After this was done, their custom was to depart and meet together again later to take food, but ordinary and harmless food.

The Odes include songs of prayer, praise, and thanksgiving, so it is completely possible that the Odes were chanted or sung for decades at sunrise gatherings like these described by Pliny or in house churches.

A number of Jewish mystic communal groups existed within the vast Syrian region. Perhaps the best known were the Essenes. That early Christians in Syria followed Essenic mystic traditions is evidenced in the writings of Tatian (c. 120 – c. 180 CE) and Theophilus (Patriarch of Antioch 169–183). Many, assuming the Dead Sea Scrolls to be a product of the Essenes, believe the Odes are so consistent with the Scrolls that the Odist was likely a Christian convert from the Essenes or from a group descended from the Essenes.

The messianic movement that originated with Jesus began in community. The first Community comprised Jesus and his immediate followers. Jesus was a mystic by virtue of His union with God and his followers were mystics by means of their union with Jesus. How then could the Odist's community of Christians continue to be mystics in communion with God and with Jesus one hundred years or more after the time of Jesus and his first disciples? The answer lies in the doctrines and practices they followed, many of which are expressed in the poetry of the Odes of Solomon.

ODES OF SOLOMON
THE MESSIANIC DRAMA

Prologue

THE PURPOSE OF THIS PROLOGUE is to introduce to you a body of ancient poetry that is some of the finest ever written. But the poems are little understood, and so they are little known and little read. My hope is that the time you spend with these poems in this translation will help to remedy that situation.

I spent two years translating the Odes of Solomon. From the beginning I knew that I would find in the Odes a record of the personal experience of one who had existed in the early years of the First Advent Age, one who had been there shortly after the human Messiah — the Anointed One — appeared, did his work, and exited the world. And I had a strong feeling that I would find in the Odes of Solomon, properly understood, the way to get across to others the spiritual potentials that were being offered in those first few generations of the messianic movement that grew around the teachings of Jesus. And that is what I found in them.

It took me two years because I had to make myself familiar with two languages that were new to me — Sahidic Coptic, the language of the Nag Hammadi Library; and Syriac, the written form of the Aramaic dialect spoken across the Middle East in the first and second centuries. And I had to learn three new alphabets: the Coptic and two forms of Syriac.

The first Ode is available only in Coptic translation. And I spent my first six months working on just that. The results astounded me and gave me the intellectual courage, and the will, to go ahead with all the other Odes in Syriac.

My intention with all these efforts is to take you on a virtual journey along what has been called The Way — The Way of God, The Way of Light, The Way of Truth, The Way of Spiritual Regeneration and Rebirth — as it was lived in the early messianic age. The path we will follow has been laid out by the poet who wrote the Odes of Solomon.

To enter the poetic world of the Odes of Solomon is to enter eternity now. The main action takes place between the poet and God — and God includes God's spoken Word, the Anointed Son of God. The secondary action is between the poet and the congregation of the holy to whom he speaks. These three — God, the poet, and the congregation of the holy — are the actors in the Odes. All the other personages in the Odes are either supporting spiritual characters or else antagonists who are mentioned in the poet's dramatic and transforming narrative in order to situate us in spiritual reality. And in the spiritual reality that the poet creates, we become the living protagonists for whom the poet models his being and to whom and for whom he speaks. The spiritual manifestations of God are our helpers, our allies, and support. The instruments of Darkness are our antagonists.

The drama unfolds here, on Earth, but the scenes are staged in spiritual time and space. Syriac has only two tenses to indicate location in time — the past and the future. The present is expressed by the present participle. Likewise is the poetic imagination that speaks through the language of the Odes. There is only a redemptive past, which belongs to Darkness, and an apocalyptic future that belongs to Light. The present belongs to action. In the Odes the poet speaks out of the past and into the future from his own personal present and, in the final few Odes, from the future Great Day of the Lord. For the poet in his poems there is no other time — no other past, no other present, and no other future. And the Odes themselves are set in no specific physical places or times. The only event the poet speaks of that coincides with an event in physical time is the coming of the Messiah. And the only specific place that corresponds to a physical place is the temple mentioned in *Ode 1* and the place of holiness mentioned in *Ode 4*, both of which appear to be references to the Jerusalem Temple. However, there are also references made to unspecified "high places of the Lord." And so we see the reason for this lack of physical specificity: the poems are set in spiritual time and spiritual space.

All good poets present to us a world. But unlike nearly all other poets, the poet of the Odes presents to us a world that is not merely individual and personal; that is, he presents a world that is not counterfeit and empty at its center. His words are words of Truth that express the thought of God. His world is full and coherent. "On high" there is Paradise, the Land of the Lord, where "the Living who do not die" dwell as God's "trees" planted and cultivated by God's hand. Below there is the abode of the dead, the place of extinction, with its primal voids and deep depths. Technically this place subsumes the Earth, one of the many "generated worlds," but the abode of the dead has its own depths deeper still below the world of Earth.

There is also an inner world. And the poet uses the traditional terms of his culture to represent the active nonphysical organs of the human psycho-spiritual anatomy. Even so, the meanings and connotations of the ancient words used by the poet are colored by the poet's spiritual culture. And these meanings and the poet's spiritual culture need to be understood if we are to understand the inner world that the poet presents to us. The translation of the Odes provided in this volume assumes that the poet's use of these traditional terms conveys teachings like those represented in the Thanksgiving Hymns of the Dead Sea Scrolls and the teachings of the amended New Covenant messianic outgrowths of these teachings, represented in the New Testament canon by the Gospel of John and Book of Revelation and in the scriptures of the Church of the East by the Gospel of Philip, the Gospel of Thomas, and related writings.

The Odes are at once personal, archetypal, and representative. This is the power of their poetry. At the center of the action there is an "I" who reports and exhorts and praises and pleads and recollects and tells stories. And this "I" has a history, but it is a spiritual history.

And this history is what makes the poems archetypal: it is the history of *a Son of God*. And the lives of Sons and Daughters of God have been very similar throughout the ages: there is always the joyous experience of personal spiritual regeneration and transformation in a physical environment of harassment and oppression. That is why the Odes are representative: they speak to, and sometimes for, every one of the holy congregation to whom they are addressed. All of "the holy" are called upon to become regenerated and transformed beings who look forward to sharing in spiritual goodness and the arrival of the Great Day of the Lord. In this respect, the poet of the Odes is acting as a sort of spiritual Walt Whitman who speaks to and for his nation; and his model for action as *a* son of God is *the* Son of God — the Beloved of God, the Anointed One, the Messiah, the human embodiment of the Word — who revived the Way (*Ode 7*) and smoothed it out to make it easier to follow for those who come after him (*Ode 22*). And because the poet himself is a Son of God (*Ode 36*), he and the Messiah, the Anointed Lord, have something in common: they both speak the Word of Truth. This is the reason why so many commentators on the Odes have not always been clear on when the "Word of Truth" in the Odes is being spoken by the poet in his persona as *a* son of God or in the persona of the Messiah, *the* Son of God.

The poet clearly identifies himself in his archetypal role and persona: He is a spiritually regenerated being (*Ode 1*) joined to the divine (*Ode 3*), a poet filled with Words of Truth (*Ode 12*) whose work it is to make the Lord's songs (*Ode 16*), a priest of the Lord (*Ode*

20) and the head of a congregation (*Ode 17*) whose own personal renown provides praise to God (*Ode 18*), who has drunk the milk of God (*Ode 19*) and received the Messiah's staff of power (*Ode 29*), who has been anointed by the perfection of the Most High (*Ode 36*), and who has been taken up into the Light of True Reality and led to the threshold of eternal Life and made wise (*Ode 38*).

The Spirit of the Lord speaks through the poet (*Ode 6*), and it is by this Spirit that the poet's thoughts are raised to the height of Truth (*Ode 17*). Sometimes the poet speaks simply as a mystic, one who receives the thought of the Lord and makes songs that express this thought (*Odes 6, 7, 12, 16, 21, 26, 37, 40*). Sometimes he speaks as a narrator of events (*Odes 6, 7, 19, 22, 23, 24, 32, 33, 39*), sometimes with exhortations to the congregation of the holy (*Odes 3, 7, 8, 9, 13, 20, 23, 30, 41*), and sometimes with petitions for the congregation, or himself, to God (*Odes 4, 5, 14, 18*). Sometimes he speaks as a Son of God who is expressing the personal and archetypal experience of dynamic spiritual transformation (*Odes 1, 3, 7, 11, 15, 17, 19, 21, 25, 27, 28, 29, 35, 36, 38*), and sometimes he speaks in the voice of the Anointed Lord, the Messiah (*Odes 8, 9, 10, 31, 42*).

The poet also addresses us. At times he addresses each of us individually, familiarly, in the second-person singular (*Odes 20, 34*). And at other times he addresses, in the second-person plural, all who are in the congregation of the holy (*Odes 3, 7, 8, 9, 13, 23, 30, 39, 41*). The poet also addresses God (*Odes 1, 4, 5, 11, 14, 18, 22, 25*), the Messiah (*Ode 17*), and Truth (*Ode 38*).

As the drama unfolds, the Odes present a sequence of personal experience and transformation — from the beginning of the poet's personal spiritual regeneration, through to the time of the great change and transformation that has begun to occur on Earth with the appearance of the Messiah, and on to the dawning of the Great Day when all the Earth begins to be restored to Light. Each individual poem, by its place in this sequence, presents the poet's thoughts and feelings at one of the stages in this dramatic transformation.

The two relatively complete copies of the Odes that have come down to us in Syriac are separated by 500 years, yet both are numbered in exactly the same sequence. And a reference by the fourth-century Roman writer Lactantius to a numbered citation in one of the Odes seems to have been made to a text written in the second century, an indication that the sequence of the Odes was set quite early, if not originally by the author. These facts are significant. The Odes are not a seamless and fully designed series of cantos like Dante's *Divine Comedy*, but the Odes tell an epic story: the personal transformation of a burgeoning Child of God in spiritual company with the promised Messiah, who had come to broaden the Way to immortal life and also to inaugurate the promised Great Day of the Lord. Some of the Odes even make indirect references to events that are supposed to have taken place in the predestined ministry of the Messiah, events that are prophesied in the Book of Isaiah and the Testament of the Twelve Patriarchs and described in the Book of Enoch: His persecution, the casting of lots over His belongings,

His crucifixion, His own resurrection, and the rising of the cosmic Sun of Righteousness at the dawn of the eternal Great Day of God.

Each Ode expresses a high point of spiritual experience or dramatic intensity, like songs in a modern American musical. And the experiences are so clear and complete that any Child of God could find in them personal meaning, if not identify with them outright. Two events set the stage of the drama: the coming of the Messiah and the coming of the Great Day of the Lord. Everything that happens in the Odes happens in relation to these two events.

Act I

THE ODES OF SOLOMON portrays a messianic drama that is played out, as I see it, in two acts, like many modern operas. Act I (*Odes 1-21*) recounts the poet's past and present processes and experiences and events of his personal transformation on the way to redemption and ascension. The action takes place sometime after the desecration and destruction of the Second Jerusalem Temple in 70 CE. The promised Messiah has already appeared on Earth, where He suffered persecution and was crucified by his enemies, and He has already been redeemed Himself. As the risen Anointed One, the Messiah is still directly accessible to the poet and the congregation. The poet has acknowledged Him as Anointed Lord, and because of this the poet has suffered persecution similar to the Messiah's as he gathers and instructs his own congregation of the holy.

The scenes of this drama are not scenes of action but stages in the process of personal spiritual regeneration and world restoration.

Even so, these stages are merely implicit in the Odes. They are not stated. The drama itself takes place in an approximation of eternity where there is a sequence of events with no specific duration. Even the action that is described in the narrative past or in the future takes place in no specific place and at no exact time.

The imagery of the Odes is drawn from nature. Yet the action that takes place in the Odes does not take place in earthly nature but in a supranatural environment where everything is an expression of the divine. We are invited to make a living crown for ourselves from the Lord's tree, so that His scion shoots may sprout within us and bring us True Realization. Gentle showers cover us with serenity and make a cloud of peace rise above our heads. Springs flow from the Lord's lips, and their speaking waters, when they touch our lips, bring the kind of inebriation that leads to knowledge and that refresh the spirit continually with their brightness and purity. God's Sun is the reservoir of His Light, and when it rises up in the Land of the Living it can be recognized by His faithful on Earth. God's Light opens our hearts, and when we put on His Light as if it were clothing, our souls have limbs.

And when we are planted in paradise, the Land of the Living, we are transformed into that Light. The imagery also is drawn from the time of Spring — the grafting of fruit trees with scion shoots, flowing springs, and surging rivers. And Spring is the traditional time to celebrate the exodus under Moses to the promised land, whose metaphor is milk and honey. Spring is also the time of renewal and regeneration, and the time of celebration of rebirth.

ACT I: SCENE 1
ENGRAFTED WITH THE DIVINE

ODE 1

The Lord is upon my head as a crown, and so I do not miss the crown that belongs to the Temple.

Bound to me, the crown brings True Realization, and has made Your scion shoot sprout deep within me,
   because a shoot is not taken for a crown when it is dried up, never to blossom,
   but it is You, alive upon my head, and You have blossomed upward over me.

Your fruit — they grow full and they ripen to perfection.
   Then, the Producer's work complete, I, Your young one, rise up triumphant.

ODE 2

[This entire Ode is lost.]

ODE 3

[An unknown number of initial lines are missing.]

. . . I am putting on, and His limbs with it.

And so I depend on them — and He is deeply attached to me — for I really would not know how to love the Lord , if He had not always shown love to me.

Who is able to discern love, if not one who is loved?

I am deeply attached to the Beloved, and my soul loves Him; and wherever His gentle calm is, there I am also.

*And I will be no stranger
to Him, because there
is no holding back with
the Lord Most High and
Compassionate.*

*I have become
intermingled with Him,
because the lover has found
the Beloved — because I, by
loving the Son, shall become
a Son:*

*whoever is truly joined
with One Who Does Not Die
will become One Who Does
Not Die,
and whoever chooses Life
will live.*

*This is the Spirit of the
Lord, who does not deceive,*

*who teaches the children of
man to know the Lord's ways.*

*Be wise and knowing and aware,
all of you.*

Hallelujah

Ode 1 has come down to us in a single third-century Egyptian translation. And what has come down to us may be only an excerpt from the whole poem. We do not know. But it is one of the most beautiful images constructed by the poet of the Odes.

The Egyptian translator of Ode 1 almost certainly translated the poem from Greek. He retained three Greek words: the word for "truth," the word for "plant shoot," and the word for "fruit," even though Coptic Egyptian equivalents existed for each of these three words. The retention of the Greek words I took to be a clue that the Egyptian translator intended to present some specialized secondary meaning of each of these words. And a search for these meanings led me to discover the beautiful metaphor these three Greek words were used to create. Together they take a common agricultural image from nature and make it into an image of spiritual culture — the grafting of fresh plant shoots onto a compatible root stock in order to rejuvenate the stock so that it produces better fruit.

Because no previous translator seems to have seen this image clearly in this poem, the translation of *Ode 1* presented here is different from previous translations — so different that it warrants some explanation. The opening statement of the poem expresses at once a sense of elevation and a sense of disassociation:

> *The Lord is upon my head as a crown,*
> *and so I do not miss the crown*
> *that belongs to the Temple.*

The poet who wrote *Ode 1* was a member of a messianic Community from sometime around the second century of our era, and so he was at a double remove in time and space from the Jerusalem temple crown. The Jerusalem Temple was destroyed in 70 CE by Roman occupation forces. The crown and other liturgical accouterments of the temple were removed from Jewish hands and never returned. Yet, because it is the Lord that is on the poet's head as a crown, the poet does not feel the pain of disassociation from the Temple crown.

(The Roman spoils of the Jerusalem temple were stored for display in Rome in the Temple of Peace, which was completed in 75 CE. The crown was reported as being seen there in the mid-second century by Rabbi Eliezer ben Jose on his visit to Rome (Babylonian Talmud *Yoma* 57a). In 455 when the spoils of the Jerusalem temple, including the crown, were seized by the Vandals, they were taken to Carthage. From there they were removed by the Byzantine general Belisarius in 534 and taken to Constantinople. It is said that Emperor Justinian sent them to a church in Jerusalem (Procopius, *Wars* iv, 9, 1–9), where they remained until the seventh century. At some later unknown date they disappeared completely.)

The second verse — *and so no longer will I be without the one from the temple* — is made of only three words in Coptic:

and + a long compound word + not

Previous translators simply followed the translation of this verse provided in 1909 by the first modern translator of the Odes, James Rendel Harris: "And I shall never be without Him." Apparently, neither Harris nor any translator after him thoroughly analyzed the unusually long compound word. But, being such an unusual construction, it is important to decode. The verse may be parsed out something like this:

and + [sign of the ablative—I—belonging to—temple—masculine pronoun—without] + not

The compound word is an ablative construction that points up the relation between the poet, the living crown, and the temple crown. The ablative case indicates that the poet does not feel disunited from the temple crown even though the temple crown is not present. This feeling tells us a lot about the messianic Community of the poet.

From the time of Aaron, the brother of Moses, the crown had represented for the people of Israel the conduit used by their high priests to connect heavenly and physical realms while the high priest himself served as a conduit to connect his people to God and God to his people. The biblical Book of Exodus provides a description of this crown and the headdress which Aaron and his successors were assigned to wear when they served God in the office of high priest. The first-century Jewish historian Josephus, who was himself the son a Jewish priest, described in detail, for his gentile readership, the elaborate headdress worn by the high priests in the Jerusalem

Temple. The image he presents is a sprouting crown: a crown of gold that surrounds the head and, sprouting above it, a golden calyx. In flowering plants, it is the calyx that protects the flower while it is in bud and supports the petals of the flower when it is in bloom. The crown of the poet is bound to him:

> *Bound to me, the crown brings*
> *True Realization, and has made*
> *Your scion shoot sprout deep within*
> *me*

Here is another parallel to the temple crown, and it draws together the grafting image of the poem even further. To form the turban of the high priest, a thin strip of linen several yards long was wound around the high priest's head, and cords were threaded through the crown to fasten it to the turban. The similarity of the headdress to scion-shoots tightly bound to the crown of the root stock in a crown graft of a fruit tree is obvious to me. I hope to make it obvious to you as well in just a moment.

But first let's take a look at a couple of the Greek loanwords. "True realization" is one of the secondary meanings of the Greek word for *truth*. Other secondary meanings are (1) true reality; (2) the true realization of a dream or omen; (3) the sapphire ornament worn by the Egyptian high priest as the symbol of truth; and (4) the oracle stone *Thummim*. The Greek word for "plant shoot" has the primary meaning of *a young slip or shoot of a tree such as is broken off for grafting*. It is translated succinctly by the English word *scion*, a word which in English also has the propitious secondary meaning of *a descendant of a notable family.*

The technique of crown grafting is practiced during the early months of Spring, the season in which spiritual resurrection has always been celebrated. The process of crown grafting is used to rejuvenate or renew fruit trees or to modify their variety. The technique is called "crown" grafting because the several grafts of scions are inserted into the topped-off root stock, the "head," all around its perimeter between the wood and the bark in a way that gives it a crown-like appearance.

In this technique, scion shoots, each carrying many well-ripened buds, are slid into the root stock and bound tightly. The tissues of the scion plant are inserted into the other so that the two sets of vascular tissue join together. For a successful graft, both tissues must be kept alive until the graft has "taken":

> *because a shoot is not taken for a crown when it is dried up, never to blossom,*

> *but it is You, alive upon my head, and You have blossomed upward over me.*

To be compatible, and to increase the success of the graft, the root stock ought to be of the same genotype as the scion. And so the agricultural metaphor extends further, and the extended metaphor enriches not only *Ode 1* but also all the references to "the root of Jesse" and "the root of Jacob" in the Book of Isaiah and similar images in the Book of Wisdom and the Book of Sirach.

Grafted trees grow and become productive faster than newly planted trees because grafted trees have the force of an established and mature root system beneath them:

> *Your fruit — they grow full and*
> *they ripen to perfection.*

The Sahidic Egyptian word for "fruit," although rarely used, does exist. Yet the Greek word is much richer in connotation than the Coptic word. It indicates not only *fruit*, but also *fruits of the earth* as well as *produce, returns, profits,* and *fulfillment.*

The final verse of the poem — which all other translators have translated following Harris's translation: "They are full of your salvation" — ends with another compound word. It is constructed of three parts:

your—young one—I rise in triumph

The theme of this last verse of the Ode is salvation:

> *Then, the Producer's work complete, I, Your young one, rise up triumphant.*

But the Egyptian word that is used to indicate salvation provides not simply the abstract idea of salvation but the actual image of salvation in the context of the poem: a young tree rising with new fruit as a result of the successful graft of the Lord's scion.

The image made in these nine verses of *Ode 1* is wonderfully dynamic: A divine scion-shoot is attached to compatible root stock through a crown graft; the divine shoot takes, sprouts, blossoms, and bears new fruit. The poet is recounting how he received into his own being the grafted shoots of divine being from the Lord's tree in the likeness of a crown that has brought him True Realization and caused him to grow, through this act of redemption, into a sapling of the Lord. It is a beautiful picture of the personal process of spiritual regeneration.

This is the kind of layering and depth and wholeness of images the poet makes throughout the entire sequence of the Odes. And because the poet is so skilled, and because the poet is inspired with what he calls the "Spirit of the Lord" and the "Word of Truth," he is able to translate his own personal spiritual transformation into completely coherent, completely full, musical spoken language, a record of the sequence of his personal development, in a way that makes the words of his poems into words that could be spoken by any of "the holy" — any of the Children of God inhabited by the

Word and experiencing a personal transformation into a Being of Light. In this way the poet is able in his poems to provide a model for all those who came after him, all those who desired to follow the Way of Light that the Messiah had come to revive. And this is no mean task.

Only two Syriac manuscripts of the Odes have come down to us. The front leaves of both manuscripts are damaged. The tenth-century manuscript begins midway into *Ode 17*. The fifteenth-century manuscript begins midway into *Ode 3*. *Ode 2* is completely lost. So is the first half of *Ode 3*. The first scene has opened with the poet engrafted with the Divine, as we have seen, an image of Springtime, an image of the poet's dynamic spiritual regeneration. He has received into his own being the grafted shoots of divine being as a crown from the Lord's tree. The narrative picks up again in the second part of *Ode 3*.

Now the Spirit of the Lord is able to speak through the poet because the poet is joined to the divine. And the poet addresses God in full recognition of what is happening to him:

> *I am deeply attached to the Beloved, and my soul loves Him* . . . .
> *And I will be no stranger to Him*
> . . . .
> *I have become intermingled with Him, because the lover has found*

> the Beloved; because I, by loving the
> Son, shall become a Son:
>> whoever is truly joined with One
>> Who Does Not Die will become One
>> Who Does Not Die
>   (ODE 3)

When the divine graft takes, one's being is renewed and regenerated and one's life takes a new direction. In the case of the poet, he has learned how to love God through His Son. Joined with God through his love of God's Son, the poet recognizes that he will also, like God's Son, become One Who Does Not Die, and so he expresses his love for the immortal Beloved One to whom he is now joined and he exhorts the congregation of the holy to wake up and become immortal themselves.

The poet is following what he comes to call "the Way of Light." And he is experiencing that Way as it is being offered in his time, and through his tradition; that is, in the spiritual company of the resurrected personal Messiah, the Anointed One, the Son of God. And through the poet's love, and through his intermingling with the Messiah, the divine being that had taken on human form, he too will become a Child of God, and a teacher, and the head of a congregation of people who also became Children of God — all modeled on the same transformation and the same experience that the Messiah had undergone. This is the experience that is laid out in sequence in the forty-two Odes.

ACT I: SCENE 2
FOLLOWING THE WAY OF LIGHT

ODE 4

No one can alter Your place of holiness, my God, and there is no one who can alter it and move it to another place,
   because no such power over it exists, for You designed Your holiness before You appointed the places.
   What is more ancient shall not be altered by things that are less than it. You have given Your heart, O Lord, to Your faithful:

Never will You cease, and never will You be without fruit,
   for one hour of Your faithfulness is worth more than all days and years.

For who was ever clothed in Your goodness and rejected?

Because Your seal is known, and Your creatures are known by it;
and Your Heavenly Powers hold it; and the Archangel Elect are clothed with it.
You have given us Your fellowship. Not that You were in need of us, but are we not always in need of You?

Shower us then with Your gentle showers, and open for us also Your increasingly growing springs that flow out milk and honey —
for with You, what is there to hold back? What should You hold back that You have promised?

Even the end was visible to You, for You also gave the means, and You gave freely. No more will You draw away and take them back again.

For all was visible to You as God, and was set out before You in order from the beginning.

And You, O Lord, made all.

Hallelujah

ODE 5

I give You thanks, O Lord, because I love You.
   O Most High, do not give up on me, because You are my hope.
   I received Your goodness freely: I will live by it.

   Any who would harass me will come and not see me
      (a cloud of dark fog will fall upon their eyes, and an air of thick fog overshadow them,
      and they will have no light to see, so they cannot take hold of me);

   their schemes will swell, turn dense as tumors, and what they devise will fall upon their own heads

(for they have thought out a scheme, and it has not come about;
　they prepared it intending evil, and found themselves unable to carry it out)

　— for my hope in the Lord is real, and I will not fear.
　And because the Lord is my salvation, I will not fear,
　for He is upon my head as a crown, and I will not be shaken.

　Even if all things are shaken, I will stand firm;
　even if all things visible perish, I will not die
　— because the Lord is with me, and I with Him.

　Hallelujah

ODE 6

Just as wind moves through the kithara and strings speak,
so does the Spirit of the Lord speak through my limbs, and so do I speak through His loving affection,
for He brings to an end whatever is foreign to Him, so that everything then is of the Lord.

This is, in fact, how it has been from the beginning, and how it will be till the end,
so that nothing will oppose Him, and nothing rise up against Him.

The Lord has magnified His knowledge, and has put out great energy so that those things that have been added to us through His goodness might be known;

and by His name He has given us His glory — Our spirits glorify His Holy Spirit!—

in fact, a stream went out and grew into a river great and wide, flowed out, indeed, over everything, and so broke everything up and carried everything to the temple;

and the barriers built by the children of man were not able to hold it back, not even the skills of those whose work it is to hold back waters,

for it spread out over the whole face of the Earth, and it filled up everything;
and all the thirsty upon Earth then drank, and thirst was relieved and put to an end,
for the drink was given from the Most High.

This is why the ministers of that drink are good, they who have been entrusted with His Water:

They have refreshed parched lips, and restored the will that had been paralyzed;
and souls near their last breath they held back from death;
and limbs that had collapsed they restored and made straight.

They gave strength by their coming, and light by their eyes;

and because of this, everyone came to know themselves in the Lord, and so lived by the Living Water of eternity.

Hallelujah

ODE 7

Just as anger runs its course over an offense, so does joy run its course over the Beloved, and it gathers in the fruits of its love with nothing to stop it.

My joy is the Lord, and my course is toward Him.

This Way of mine is beautiful. And there is even someone to help me: It is the Lord.

With no hesitation, He has made Himself known to me in His simpleness. His sweet kindness, in fact, has made it possible to bear His majesty.

He became like me; and

*because of this, I could
receive Him. In appearance He
looked like me; and because
of this, I could clothe myself
with Him.*

*And I was not shaken
when I saw Him. Because He
had come to exist, He had
compassion for me.*
   *He took on a nature like
mine; and because of this,
I could learn to understand
Him; and an image like mine;
and because of this, I need not
turn from Him.*

   *The Father of knowledge is
the Word of knowledge:*
   *He who created wisdom is
wiser than His works;*
   *and He who created me
when I did not yet exist knew*

what I would do when I did come to exist,

because He had compassion for me in His great goodness, and He allowed me to request, and to receive from Him, His offering.

And because He exists — He, the indestructible, the fullness of the generated worlds and their Father —

He has allowed Himself to be seen by those who are His own;

and because of this, they could recognize Him who made them, and not suppose that they had come of themselves, self-generated.

For it is toward knowledge that He laid out His Way: He

widened it and extended it and brought it to completion; and He laid upon it the trackways of His Light;

    and now the Way went from the beginning to the end, for He had been served by the Light, and the Light has now been revived with the Son.

And because of the Son's redemption, the Son will take possession of all, and the Most High will be acknowledged by His holy ones

    to announce to those who have songs for the Lord's coming

    that they may go out to meet Him and sing for Him, with joy and with the kithara of many tones.

The seers will go before Him, and will be seen before Him;

and they will glorify the Lord with praise in deep affection for Him, because He is close by and sees;

and so hatred will be removed from the Earth, and will be drowned out along with spite,

for whatever on Earth is not knowledge will have been destroyed, because on it will have spread the knowledge of the Lord.

Those who make songs will sing the goodness of the Lord Most High, and will offer their songs,

and their heart will be like the day, and their gentle

sounds like the majestic beauty of the Lord;

and there will be none without a soul, and none with no knowledge, and none that is silent,

for He has given mouth to His creation, to open toward Him the sound of their mouth and increase His glory.

Make known then His strength, and proclaim His goodness, all of you.

Hallelujah

ODE 8

"Open your hearts, all of you, open them to the joyous dance of the Lord, and your deep affection will grow from heart to lips

to bear fruit to the Lord, a holy Life, and to speak with awareness in His Light.

Rise up exalted and stand up straight, all you who were sometimes put down.

All you who were silenced, speak: Your mouth has been opened.

All you who were despised, be uplifted from this moment on: Your righteousness has been uplifted.

The right hand of the Lord is with you, and has been a helper for you,
   and peace has been made ready for you, even before your battle has come to be.

All of you, hear the Word of True Realization, and receive the knowledge of the Most High,
   although your flesh may not comprehend what I am about to say to you, nor your coat of skin what I am about to make known to you:

Hold to My mystery, all you who are held by it; hold to My faithfulness, all you who are held by it;
   and recognize My knowledge, all you who truly recognize Me; love Me with

deep affection, you who love Me —

for I do not turn My face from My own, because I recognize them.

They did not yet even exist when I acknowledged them and I imprinted their persons.

I made their limbs; and I made ready My own breasts for them, so they might drink My holy milk and, by it, live.

I have chosen them, and am not disgraced by them,

for they show My work, and the power of My thoughts.

And so who then will stand against My work? Or who is he who will not listen to them?

I longed for and formed mind and heart, and they are Mine.

And I have set My Elect at My own right hand, and My righteousness goes before them;

and they will not be separated from My name, because it is with them.

Seek and grow greater, and remain in the love of the Lord
— even as the loved ones in the Loved One, and as the ones held in the Living One, and so as the ones redeemed in the One redeemed.

And then, will you not be found indestructible in all ages, known by your Father's name?"

Hallelujah

ODE 9

"Open your ears, and I will speak to you.

Give me your Self, so that I may give you My Self also:

*the Word of the Lord
and His intentions, the holy
thought He has thought about
His Anointed One,*
  *for your life exists through
the Lord's intention, and His
purpose is Life eternal, and
that your fullness not perish.*

*Be rich in God the Father,
and collect the purpose of the
Most High: Be strong and be
redeemed — pay the ransom
with His goodness.*

To you all, His reconciled ones, I announce peace, so that none who hear will fall in battle;
and also that none who have known Him will perish; and so that none who will receive Him will be disgraced.

True Realization is an eternal crown (they who put it on their head are made good),
a precious stone (for battles have been fought because of that crown),
and yet righteousness has taken it, and given it to you.

Put on the crown in the true covenant of the Lord, since all those who have been victorious will be recorded in His book (for their book, the reward of victory, is also for you), and victory sees you before her and longs for you to be redeemed."

Hallelujah

ODE 10

"The Lord has made My mouth talk straight with His spoken Word, and so has opened My heart by His Light;

and He made dwell in Me His Life That Does Not Die, and permitted Me to speak the fruit of His peace

to bring back the souls of those who desire to come to Him, and so to capture those held captive, to bring them to freedom.

I was empowered and became strong, and I captured the world; and so the capture became Mine to the glory of the Most High, and of God, My Father.

And the peoples that had been scattered were gathered together; and I have not been made impure by My deep affection for them,

because they gave Me thanks in the high places, and the trackways of Light had been laid upon their heart;

and they walked in My Life and were redeemed, and so they became My people for ever and ever."

Hallelujah

The word *Hallelujah* — "Praise to God" — appears as a final exhortation at the end of each poem. Ending each poem in this way brings each poem into the action, along with the congregation the poet is speaking to. Some form of this word, or a word like it, is used in Judaic, Christian, and Muslim tradition. It is the second-person imperative plural addressed to a congregation of people and urging them to praise God.

In at least one school of the Kabbalah, the spirit is believed to be generated from *Jah*, that is, from the unknown God, a celestial state or world above the physical world. In the poetry of the Hebrew Bible, the word *Jah* appears several times by itself as a divine name. But the Aramaic word for God is *Elah*, and it is this word for God that appears in the texts of the Odes and in the biblical books Ezra, Daniel, and Jeremiah. The root meaning of the word is related to "reverence." And the name *Elah* is related to the word *Allah* — the Arabic word for "the God." The word "holy" in Aramaic is derived from the word *Elah* and can also mean "godly," "godlike," "sacred," and "divine." It is the word that is found so often in the Odes as a designation for the assembly the poet is addressing — *the holy*.

It is on behalf of the whole congregation of the holy that the poet speaks in *Ode 4*. This is the congregation of the holy the poet has appealed in *Ode 3* to wake up and undertake the process of spiritual regeneration.

In the first line of this poem, the poet speaks in recognition of the ill-conceived attempts by humankind to alter a holy place appointed by God. But it is not clear what *the place of holiness* might be. At first you may think it is a reference to an earlier alternative sanctuary to the Jerusalem temple; for example, the Samaritan temple on Mt. Gerizim that was destroyed in 128 BCE, or the sanctuary at Assouan, Egypt, that was destroyed in the sixth century BCE, or the temple of Onias at Leontopolis, Egypt, that was destroyed in 73 CE, but the image of an alternate sanctuary does not fit the dynamic of the poem.

The Syriac word *atra* that is translated here as *place* can mean more than just a region or locale. It can also mean a place where something happens, such as a ritual or liturgical space. Metaphorically, the word suggests a special place or special time of opportunity, someplace where things happen in God's time. If the line is a reference to the Jerusalem temple, which I think it is, then the message is that there can be no other temple elsewhere unless it is appointed by God. Even so, the poet tells us, the heart of God remains with the faithful.

The poet attempts to appease or console the sense of loss carried in the opening lines with the explanation that is his poem. Before the congregation, the poet speaks to God on behalf of himself and the holy congregation in recognition of what God has done for them all, even though the place of holiness is no longer available to them, as they prepare to make their way in faith and hope to the new promised land. God provides them with His faithfulness and has clothed them in the goodness that is His seal. God's seal, well-known, identifies all who are associated with Him — creatures, heavenly powers, and the archangel elect. And it is important to remember that in the age that the Odes were written, it is necessary to have the imprint of the right seal in order to travel without peril. This is the purpose of God's seal: to give them clearance to travel on their spiritual path through all obstacles.

As the holy prepare to make their way, the poet also asks that God make available to them His Living Waters, which *flow out milk and honey*, because of their need. The image of milk and honey always recalls the first Exodus from Egypt to the promised land of Canaan, a land which flows with milk and honey. Here in *Ode 4*, the image carries the promise of a new exodus, after the destruction of the temple, to a new promised land, the promised spiritual land of The Living Who Do Not Die. Certain early church bodies used milk and honey in their eucharistic rites — the followers of Bardaisan in Edessa, for example.

Then, in soliloquy, the poet in *Ode 5* gives thanks to God and expresses his trust in God, even though he stands in danger of being attacked, because God is with him as a crown upon his head.

In *Ode 6* the kithara is mentioned for the first time. The Greek kithara is a seven-stringed musical instrument, the ancestor of the modern guitar, suited for virtuoso performance by professional musician-singers. A musician made music with the instrument by stroking the plectrum in his right hand across the strings while regulating the sound of the strings with the left hand. Making music with the plectrum is the "work" the poet later refers to in the first line of *Ode 16*. The instrument appears again in *Odes 7, 14,* and *26*.

There is something else about ancient Greek music that may help to imagine how these Odes may have originally sounded when they were performed. The ancient odes of the Greeks were "through composed." Each line of text had its own melody to go with it. Melody was made to fit the words, not the other way around. What was important was not the melody itself but how the melody came through the singer and how the melody augmented the singer's words and added a new dimension to the performance.

In *Ode 6* the Spirit of the Lord, who spoke through the poet in *Ode 3*, speaks again, this time through the poet's limbs as he plays, and as the poet speaks through the Lord's loving affection about the knowledge and glory of God, narrating events that are occurring and are to come. The poet describes to the holy congregation the energy that the Lord God has put forth to make known what He has given to them. The image of the Living Waters of glory that flood the Earth to cleanse it and to help everyone know themselves in the Lord makes clear the purpose of God's ministry and how the Lord God "brings to an end whatever is foreign to Him, so that everything then is of the Lord."

The next Ode, a poem about The Way, opens quite appropriately with the image of courses being run. The poet contrasts and compares the course of anger and the course of joy with his own course. The remainder of the poem tells how the poet's course, the beautiful Way of the Lord, was constructed and revived, and how it is to be used. The Way, now modified from the equivalent of a footpath for the few to a broad highway for the many, is completely laid out with the ancient trackways — the ancient spiritual routes of those who followed the Teachings of Light and left a trail for others to follow, a set of cultural and psychic impressions, like footprints — so that the holy of all ancient traditions of Light may follow it. And to celebrate that the Light has been revived by His Son, the Messiah, a procession of seers goes before the Anointed One to announce Him and He is met by singers who go out to sing for Him.

Three songs for the Messiah follow, sung in the voice of the Messiah. The first song, *Ode 8*, is a reveille in which the Anointed One addresses the entire holy congregation. The Messiah gives the holy their instructions — to open their hearts and live uprightly — and tells them who they are — the preordained, imprinted with the divine before they even came into existence — so that they may grow out of their *coat of skin* into redemption.

The calling out continues in the second song, *Ode 9*. Here, for the first time, war is announced, and peace. And the Messiah again addresses the entire holy congregation, those who are reconciled with God or atoned, to tell them how they may acquire the crown of True Realization and so win spiritual victory. In the poem, the crown is called *True Realization* and *a precious stone*. It is the same crown spoken of in *Ode 1*.

In the third song, *Ode 10*, the Messiah tells the how and why of His ministry on Earth, and how all the various peoples of the Earth who had followed their respective traditions, *the trackways of Light*, and who now recognize Him as Anointed Lord, have been redeemed and have become His people.

ACT I: SCENE 3
RENEWED BY THE LIGHT

ODE 11

My heart has been pruned and its flower has appeared, and so goodness has sprouted up in it, and my heart has borne fruit for the Lord.

For the Most High had pruned around me through His Holy Spirit, and so laid open toward Him my innermost being, and so filled me with His deep affection.

And so His pruning around me became my salvation; and I made my way quickly in His peace, along the Way of True Realization.

From the beginning to the end, I received His knowledge,
   and I was established solidly on the rock of True Reality, the solid rock where He had set me up;
   and speaking waters touched my lips from the spring of the Lord, which does not hold back,
   and I drank and became drunk from the Living Water That Does Not Die.

   And my drunkenness was not the kind that does not lead to knowledge. Did I not leave behind useless things?
   And I turned back toward the Most High, my God, and I was made rich by His gift of goodness.

And I left behind the foolishness that is broadcast upon the Earth, and then I took it off and cast it away from me.
And the Lord renewed me with His raiment, and so acquired me with His Light;

and from above He revived me with what cannot be corrupted, and so I became like a land that blossoms and laughs in its fruits,
and the Lord became like the Sun upon the face of the land.

My eyes lit up, and my countenance collected the dew,
and my breath laughed with the sweet fragrance of the Lord.

And He led me away into His paradise, where is the wealth of the Lord's delight.
And I revered the Lord because of His glorious radiance.

And I said, "They are good, O Lord, are they not, those who are planted in Your land, and have a place in Your paradise,
and who sprout up in Your trees' sprouting growth, and have transformed from Darkness to Light?

See, all Your laborers are beautiful, they who work good works, and turn away from what is useless toward Your sweetness.

And by themselves the trees have changed from bitterness, once they were planted in Your land;

and they all exist as a remnant of You, and an eternal remembrance of Your faithful servants.

How great is the space in Your paradise! And what place in it lies idle? Is it not all filled with fruit?

Radiant splendor is Yours, O God, the everlasting delight of paradise!"

Hallelujah

ODE 12

By the Word I am made full of Truth, so that I may speak the Word.

And like the flow of water flows Truth from my mouth, and the fruits of the Word take shape upon my lips.

And the Word has magnified its knowledge in me, because the True Word is the utterance of the mouth of the Lord, and the gateway of His Light.

And the Most High gave the Word also to His generated worlds; and they are the interpreters of His beauty, and so the reporters of His glory,

and the revealers of His plan, and so the messengers

of His thought, and so the teachers of what He has made.

And yet no narrative can express the subtlety of the Word; and any utterance of it has its same subtlety and sharpness, and so there is no end to its continual unfolding.

And it does not lose its power, and it does not lose its course. And its descent, and the way it takes, cannot be comprehended.

For what it does is like the result that it expects, for it is the light and the dawning of thought;

and by it the generated worlds spoke one to another, and those that were silent learned how to speak;

and from it came the friendship of love and the

equality of concord, and they spoke one to another whatever they had to say.

And they were urged on by the Word, and so they came to know Him who made them, in the equality of concord,
  because it was the mouth of the Most High that spoke to them, and through the Word His exposition accomplished His work,
  for the habitation of the Word is man, and affectionate love is its Truth.

They are good who by means of it have understood everything, and recognized the Lord in His Truth.

  Hallelujah

ODE 13

See, the Lord is our mirror:
Open your eyes in Him, all
of you, and look at them,
   and then learn the real look
of your face, and send praises
of its glory to His Spirit;
   and wipe the anguish
from your face, and love His
holiness and put it on,
   and with Him you will never
have a blemish for all time.

Hallelujah

The scene cuts to the spiritual renewal of the poet, and the intimate circumstances of the poet's own transformation are revealed.

> *My heart has been pruned and its flower has appeared, and so goodness has sprouted up in it. . . .*
> *For the Most High had pruned around me . . . and so laid open toward Him my innermost being. . . .*
> (ODE 11)

In *Ode 1* the divine has been grafted onto the crown of the earthly rootstock so that the earthly tree will produce spiritual fruit. In *Ode 11* the grafted "tree," the poet himself, is pruned so that his innermost being is laid open to the Lord to produce more yield, and he takes in the radiations of the Sun like a young tree. The process of pruning that made this possible initiates the assimilation of the energy and intelligence carried by this Light, and this energy and intelligence influences the poet to think and act in such a way that God's Light shines favorably upon him and makes him more receptive to receive it.

Just as the songs sung by the singers in *Ode 7* had promised, the poet's soul is opened and he receives knowledge. In *Ode 11* the poet recounts the feelings and sensations of his own process of transformation as he matured "along the Way of True Realization," the Way that the Messiah spoke of in *Odes 8* and *9*.

Renewed by Light and looking upon the Spiritual Sun, the poet is led by God into a vision of paradise. There he sees those who have been planted in the Lord's Land of the Living and how they have been transformed by being planted there, and to God he praises the radiant beauty of the place.

When we learn to stop listening to that inner self, the Dark Self, and we begin to follow the Way of God and to grow in spirit, and we look upon the Sun in this condition, our minds are linked with the mind of God. This is what is meant by the incarnation of the Word in Man. And the poet describes the experience.

In *Ode 12* the poet, now filled with God's Word, opens up. And the generated worlds first mentioned in *Ode 7* again come into the picture. They are in fact the main receivers and agents of the energy and inspiration of God's Word. The poet, filled by the Word with words of Truth, is able to expound upon the nature and workings of the Word in the generated worlds.

The poet then urges all the holy congregation, all those who by means of the Word have understood everything, to see their true face in God.

ACT I: SCENE 4
FILLED WITH GOD'S WORD

ODE 14

Like the eyes of a son on his father, like this are my eyes always toward You, O Lord,
   because with You are the breasts of my nourishment and my delight.

Do not turn Your compassion from me, O Lord, and do not take from me Your sweet kindness;
   reach out to me, O Lord, Your right hand always, and so by Your Will be my guide to the end.

I will be beautiful before You because of Your glory; and because of Your name, I will be redeemed from the Evil One;

and Your repose, O Lord, will live within me, and also the fruits of Your affection.

Teach me the odes of Your Truth, so that I may bear fruit in You;

and open for me the kithara of Your Holy Spirit, so that I, with every tone, may increase Your glory, O Lord.

And You will grant me as much as the multitude of Your compassionate feelings, and that much do You hurry to grant our appeals.

And You are able to meet all our needs.

Hallelujah

ODE 15

Just as the Sun is the joy of those who seek its day, so is my joy the Lord,
   because He is my Sun, and His rays have awakened me, and His Light has dispelled all Darkness from my face.

Through Him I have acquired eyes, and so I have seen His Holy Day;
   I have ears, and I have heard His Truth;

I have had the thoughts that come with understanding, and have lived in delight by His hand;
   I have put aside the way of

error, and I have gone to Him and received redemption from Him with no hesitation.

And He gave me a gift that is divine like His own, and He made me a beauty that is sublime like His own:
By means of His name, I have put on what cannot be destroyed; and by means of His goodness, I have taken off what can be destroyed.

Death itself was destroyed in my presence; and then, at my spoken Word, the abode of the dead was made to cease.
And so my Sun rose up in the Land of the Lord, the Living That Do Not Die, and it was acknowledged by His

faithful; and it was given, lacking nothing, to those who trust in Him.

Hallelujah

ODE 16

Like the work of a farmer with the blade of a plough, and the work of a helmsman with the rudder of a ship, so is my work with the plectrum of the Lord in the hymns of His praise.

My craft and my service are in His praise, because His deep affection has nourished my heart, and has poured out His fruits unto my lips,
   for my deep affection is for the Lord, and so I will sing to Him;
   I am strengthened, in fact, through praising Him, and through Him I have faith.

I will open my mouth, and through me His Spirit will speak — of the glory of the Lord and His beauty,
  of the work of His hands, and the movements of His fingers,
  of the multitude of His compassion, and the driving power of His speech.

For the speech of the Lord traces out what is not visible, and reveals His thought,
  so that the eye sees His works, and the ear hears His thought.

The Word has spread the Earth out wide, and made water travel through the seas,
  stretched out the heavens, and set in order the stars,

*and put the things it created
in order and set them up to
last. Then it rested from its
works.*

*And the created things run
as they run, and so work their
work, and they do not know
how to stop and so they do
not cease;
   and even the Powers
are subject to His speech.*

*The reservoir of light is
the Sun, and the reservoir of
darkness is the night;
   but the Word has made the
Sun for day so that it is bright,
then night carries darkness
over the face of the Earth;
   and by their receiving
of one from the other, they
complete God's beauty.*

And what is there that is outside the Lord? Because before everything came into existence, He was.

Even the generated worlds came to exist by His speech, and so by the thought of His heart.

Glory and honor to His name!

Hallelujah

With the coming of God's Thought into the world at the dawning of God's Great Day, the poet recognizes that the Light of God is his nourishment.

> *Like the eyes of a son on his father, like this are my eyes always toward You, O Lord,*
> *because with You are the breasts of my nourishment and my delight.*
> (ODE 14)

With the kithara of the Holy Spirit again beside him, the poet looks upon God and petitions Him to teach him His Odes, so that he may bear fruit for God by the singing of them.

The poet's petition is answered, and he sings of his own personal awakening and transformation as he looks upon God's Sun, whose Light has allowed him to see God's Holy Day. He tells how he became receptive to God's divine gifts and how he acquired the Life That Does Not Die.

> *Just as the Sun is the joy of those who seek its day, so is my joy the Lord,*
> *because He is my Sun, and His rays have awakened me, and His Light has dispelled all Darkness from my face.*

> *Through Him I have acquired eyes, and so I have seen His Holy Day;*
>
> *I have ears, and I have heard His Truth;*
>
> *I have had the thoughts that come with understanding, and have lived in delight by His hand. . . .*
>
> (ODE 15)

The poem ends with God's Sun rising in the Land of the Living and His faithful acknowledging it.

As we turn our eyes toward the physical sun, we look for this other Sun, the Sun behind the Sun, to appear.

> *And so my Sun rose up in the Land of the Lord, the Living That Do Not Die, and it was acknowledged by His faithful; and it was given, lacking nothing, to those who trust in Him.*
>
> (ODE 15)

The spiritual Light Body responds to the radiations of this messianic Sun, just as the material body and the solar body under the influence of Darkness respond to the physical and psychic radiations from the cosmic Sun of our world. The poet's experience of the Light of the Spiritual Sun and its effects upon him are expressed throughout the sequence of Odes in this scene. First as a hope.

> *I will be beautiful before You because of Your glory; and because of Your name, I will be redeemed from the Evil One . . .*
> (ODE 14)

And later as a reality.

> *And He gave me a gift that is divine like His own, and He made me a beauty that is sublime like His own:*
> *By means of His name, I have put on what cannot be destroyed; and by means of His goodness, I have taken off what can be destroyed.*
> (ODE 15)

The poet knows as well that this Light is filled with divine Thought.

> *For the speech of the Lord traces out what is not visible, and reveals His thought,*
>
> *so that the eye sees His works, and the ear hears His thought.*
>
> (ODE 16)

The poet, now recognizing that his craft and his service is in speaking praise of the workings of the Lord God, and with the kithara of the Lord in hand, describes his art in singing his love for the Lord. The act strengthens him, and he goes on to sing praises of the Lord and His Word as he goes to work with the plectrum of the Lord.

The Syriac word translated as *plectrum* is the common word for psalm. But because the root of the Greek word *psalm* is "pluck," I translated it as *plectrum*, the tool of the psalmist, to emphasize the poet's clever parallel of the psalmist's tool, the plectrum, with the farmer's plough blade and the helmsman's rudder.

ACT I: SCENE 5
TRANSFORMED INTO LIGHT

ODE 17

*I have been crowned —
but by my God — and so my
crown is a living one.
And I was shown to be
righteous by my Lord; my
redemption, therefore, cannot
perish.*

*I have been released from
useless things, and so I do not
stand condemned.
My ties were severed by
His hands. I took on the face
and form of a new person;
and I walked in it, and I was
redeemed.*

*And the thought of True
Reality led me onward; and
I went after it, and I did not
wander.*

And all who saw me were astounded; and to them I seemed like an alien,
  except for the one who knew me and made me great — the Most High in all His fullness.

And through His sweet kindness He increased my glory, and raised my mind to the height of True Realization;
  and from there He put me on the pathway of His steps;
  and I opened the gates that had been locked shut,
  and I shattered the iron bars of distorted perception — my own irons glowed and dissolved before me!

And now nothing at all seemed shut to me, because I was the opening of all.

And I approached all those who had been shut in with me to release them, leaving no one shut in or shutting in others;

and I gave my knowledge with no holding back, and my consolation came through my deep affection;

and I planted the seeds of my fruits in their hearts, and transformed them through me.

And they received my blessing and lived; and they were gathered to me and were redeemed,

because they had become my limbs, and I was their head.

*Glory to You, our head,
Anointed Lord!*

Hallelujah

ODE 18

My heart was lifted up by the Most High's affection — and made greater — so I might increase His glory with my own renown.

My limbs were made stronger, as if they would never fall from His power;

weakness ran out of my body, and my limbs stood firm in the Lord through His Will, because His Kingdom stands firm.

O Lord, because of the needs of those who are lacking, keep with me Your Word;

do not, because of their deeds, deny me Your fullness,

nor let Light be defeated by Darkness, nor Truth run away from falsehood.

Your right hand will bring our redemption to victory, and gather it from all places, and protect on all sides those laid siege by evils.

You, my God — falsehood and death are outside Your mouth; nothing but fullness is Your Will;

and so emptiness is a thing You do not know, because it does not know You,

and You do not know error, because it does not know You either.

And whatever is not knowledge has a look like blinding spray, and like scum washed up by the sea;

and yet empty people have supposed it was great, and so they followed its example and became empty nothingness.

But those who understand understood and thought things out, and they were not polluted by their thoughts, because they were in the mind of the Most High;
and they laughed off those who were walking in error; and they also spoke Truth, from the breath which the Most High breathed into them.

Glory and greatness to His name!

Hallelujah

ODE 19

A cup of milk was given me, and I drank it in the sweetness of the Lord's kindness.
The Son is the cup; and the one who was milked, the Father; and the one who milked Him, the Spirit of Holiness.

Because His breasts were full, and it was not wanted that His milk be released without being used,
the Spirit of Holiness opened the matrix of Her bosom, and mixed the milk of the two breasts of the Father;
and She gave the intimate commingling to the beings of the generated worlds without

their knowing; and those who take it are in the fullness of the right hand.

The womb of the Virgin took it, and She conceived and gave birth.
And so the Virgin became a mother with great feelings of compassion.

And She went into labor and gave birth to the Son, but not with pain, because nothing happened that had no use.
And She did not call for a midwife, because it was the Father who had given the life.

Like a strong man, She gave birth with a sense of will, and She gave birth with a sense of making Him known, and so She had Him with a sense of great power;

  and yet She expressed deep affection with a sense of redemption, and protected Him with a sense of kindness, and presented Him with a sense of majesty.

  Hallelujah

ODE 20

*I am a priest of the Lord,
and I serve Him as priest.*
   *And to Him I offer the
offering of His thought*
   *— for His thought is not like
the thought of the world, nor is
it like the thought of the flesh,
nor is it like the thought of
those who serve the flesh —*
   *the offering of the Lord is
righteousness, and purity of
heart and lips.*

   *Offer your innermost being
with no blemish; and so do
not let your feelings put down
the feelings of another, and
do not let your soul put down
another's soul;*

neither should you make a stranger a slave, for his soul is blood kin to your own; and never try to deceive one who is close to you, and never take from him the covering of his nakedness.

Instead, put on the goodness of the Lord with no holding back, and enter into His paradise;
and then make for yourself a crown from His tree; and put it on your head and laugh, and trust in His repose.
And in this way His glory will go before you, and you will receive His kindness and His goodness, and you will be filled out with Truth in the glory of His reconciliation.

Glory and honor to His name!

Hallelujah

ODE 21

*I raised my arms on high to the compassion of the Lord,
because He cast aside the chains that had bound me,
and my helper raised me up through His compassion and His redemption.*

*And I took off Darkness, and I clothed myself with Light;
and then I had limbs for my soul, in which there was no pain, nor sickness, nor suffering.*

But my greatest gain was the help of the Lord's thought, and His fellowship with me, which is indestructible.

And I was raised up into the Light, and I passed before His face,
   and so I was close to Him, while I sang praises of glory and gave thanks to Him.

My heart welled up and found itself in my mouth, and then there rose upon my lips,
   and then there grew upon my face, the joyous dance of the Lord together with His glory.

Hallelujah

In the first line of *Ode 17* there is a verbal particle that other translators have either discounted as a "poetic" or "empty" word, or else translated as "then." I think the poet used the word to true poetic purpose, which is to say, for emphasis, and so I have translated the line *I have been crowned — but by my God.*

This crowning goes back directly to the crown grafting image of *Ode 1*. In this poem, the poet recounts the life that followed this life-changing transformation. Everything is changed. The singer speaks as one of the Living, a Son of God. He tells the whole story of how he was grafted with the divine and transformed, how he worked to transform others, how those others received his endowment and Lived and became strong *limbs* grown from this grafting, and how he became their *head*.

The Syriac word *hnaqe*, meaning "bands" or "bonds," I have translated as "ties" in the line *My ties were severed by his hands.* The word is used only in this particular Ode. The root of the word indicates choking or strangling. A closely related word indicates the strings or bands of a yoke that tie around the neck. In addition to the general image of liberation in this line, I see the image of spiritual horticulture from *Ode 1* appear again — this time in the cutting of the bands that hold a new graft in place once the graft has "taken."

On the road to reconciliation with God, the poet has come to recognize that with his crowning by God he has been proven righteous, and he sings of his transformation and the alterations that have affected his thinking processes. His mind, illuminated with thoughts that have their origin outside of this world, begins to remember, to experience, and to think on a higher level.

> *And through His sweet kindness He increased my glory, and raised my mind to the height of True Realization;*
> *and from there He put me on the pathway of His steps; and I opened the gates that had been locked shut,*
> *and I shattered the iron bars of distorted perception....*
> (ODE 17)

The process of transformation that raised the poet's mind "to the height of True Realization" has freed him from distorted perception and so made him able to free others with his knowledge. It is by taking action through this freedom that he has become their head. And he acts on behalf of the congregation that he has gathered around himself — just as the Temple priest of the Old Covenant in earlier times, who wore the Temple crown, had acted as a spiritual conduit for his people. In a final flourish, the poet, the head of the congregation he has freed, praises the head of them all: the Lord Messiah.

The poet tells how all the systems at work in his body were altered in the transformation he experienced, his being flooded with cosmic energies that originate in worlds beyond his own.

> *My heart was lifted up by the Most High's affection — and made greater — so I might increase His glory with my own renown.*
>
> *My limbs were made stronger, as if they would never fall from His power;*
>
> *weakness ran out of my body, and my limbs stood firm in the Lord through His Will, because His Kingdom stands firm.*
>
> (ODE 18)

Then the poet, the head of the congregation whose story is told in *Ode 17*, speaks to God <u>as</u> its head. He petitions God on behalf of his congregation to keep the Word with him so that he may be able to help others, "those who are lacking," even despite their misdeeds. And his petition turns into a paean to God's knowledge and Truth.

As the new state of the world approaches, the poet tells the means by which he received the spiritual nourishment that sustains him.

> *The Son is the cup; and the one who was milked, the Father; and the one who milked Him, the Spirit of Holiness.*
>
> (ODE 19)

And he provides a narrative of the spiritual mystery that had occurred in order for this nourishment to be produced and offered.

> *Because His breasts were full,*
> *and it was not wanted that His milk*
> *be released without being used,*
>> *the Spirit of Holiness opened*
>> *the matrix of Her bosom, and mixed*
>> *the milk of the two breasts of the*
>> *Father;*
>> *and She gave the intimate commingling to the beings of the generated worlds without their knowing; and those who take it are in the fullness of the right hand.*
>
> (ODE 19)

The difficult word is *ubba*. This is the Syriac word for "bosom" as well as lap, womb, and matrix. Translating the word, I did not want to lose the sense of bosom, so appropriate to the discussion of milk and breasts. Neither did I want to miss the fertile biological sense of matrix — an environment in which something develops — nor the mathematical sense — an organizational structure in which two or more lines of communication may run through the same individual. I tried to get it all with the phrase *matrix of Her bosom*. The whole story told in the poem in archetypal fashion can be interpreted both as an explanation of the "virgin birth" of the Anointed One as well as the process of spiritual conception and birth by which the Virgin, Goodness, comes to bear every Child of God.

In the stories of the Patriarchs, the primeval feminine aspect of deity, Shaddai, is linked to fertility. The blessing of Shaddai brings fruitfulness and many children (Genesis 28:3, 35:11; 48:3-4). El Shaddai blesses with blessings from heaven above and from the deep beneath, from the breasts and from the matrix of her womb (Genesis 49:25) as the Spirit of Holiness does in this poem. Yet whenever this male/female breasted deity reappears in early Christian hymns, as it has in *Ode 19*, it is commonly identified as a textual problem or else evidence of Hindu influence rather than as a fascinating piece of evidence for the survival of Shaddai in the image of the Holy Spirit.

In *Ode 20*, for the first time in the series, the poet speaks in the more intimate second-person singular (you) rather than the second-person plural (all of you). Now a priest of the Lord God, the poet instructs each of the holy to put on the goodness of God and to offer their beings to God with no blemish.

In the process of spiritual transformation, what is first activated and actualized is the ancient psychic self that we all are, <u>each peculiar to itself</u>. This is the archetypal Self, that Dark person who is very knowledgeable and which is sometimes called the Devil or Satan. And in the beginning of this process, that inner self begins to speak to us and to guide us down the wrong path. As might be expected, the poet did not celebrate this stage. But he did recognize it.

> *... Did I not leave behind useless things?*
>
> *And I turned back toward the Most High, my God, and I was made rich by His gift of goodness.*
>
> (ODE 11)

And once the poet learned to stop listening to that inner self, the Dark Self, he began to follow the Way of God and to grow in spirit.

> *I have put aside the way of error, and I have gone to Him and received redemption from Him with no hesitation.*
>
> (ODE 15)

And the putting off of this Dark Nature is what he celebrates.

> *I have been released from useless things, and so I do not stand condemned.*
>
> *My ties were severed by His hands. I took on the face and form of a new person; and I walked in it, and I was redeemed.*

> *And the thought of True Reality*
> *led me onward; and I went after it,*
> *and I did not wander.*
> (ODE 17)

At the end of this process, the poet is prepared to face God.

> *And I took off Darkness, and I*
> *clothed myself with Light;*
> *and then I had limbs for my soul,*
> *in which there was no pain, nor*
> *sickness, nor suffering.*
> (ODE 21)

In *Ode 21* the poet, as one who received the Lord's goodness and has grown full in Truth, tells how he was raised up into the Light and passed before God's face while he *sang praises of glory and gave thanks to Him.*

At the end of the poem, the joyous dance of the Lord Messiah is invoked, not in bodily leaps for joy, nor in a leaping heart as in *Ode 28*, nor in the leaps of the joyous spirit as in *Ode 40*, but in his smile and the poetic leaps of speech that the poet speaks out next in *Ode 22*.

The poet's ascent into the Light marks a spiritual change of state. It is the central event in the sequence of poems. With his ascent, ACT I ends.

Act II

ACT II, THE SECOND HALF OF THE SERIES, brings the future into the present. *Odes 22–42* envelop the processes and events of the restoration that occur with the coming of the Great Day of the Lord. Once the poet has been clothed in Light, his reality is changed. His personal redemption and transformation complete, he now teaches as one of the Living. From this moment on, his recollections and narratives are truly universal. All that he sees and experiences are primordial scenes with primordial actors.

ACT II: SCENE 1
WALKING IN KNOWLEDGE OF GOD'S THOUGHT

ODE 22

The One who sent me down from on high, and brought me up from below,

and the One who gathers those in my midst, and joins them to me,

the One who scattered my enemies, and those who opposed me,

the One who gave me power over chains, so that I could release them,

the One who by my hands overthrew the serpent with seven heads, and set me at its roots so I could destroy its seed

— You were there and helped me, and everywhere Your name surrounded me for defense.

Your right hand wrung out the serpent's evil venom; and Your hand smoothed out for Your faithful what was not level on the Way,
    even chose them from graves, and separated them from those that were dead:
    it took dead bones, and overlaid them with bodies,
    and when they did not move, even gave them energy for Life.

The indestructible — that is Your Way and Your presence. You brought the generated world to destruction,
    so that everything could be dissolved and renewed, and Your stone could be the foundation of everything;
    and so upon it You built

Your Kingdom, and so it became the habitation of the holy.

Hallelujah

ODE 23

Joy is for the holy, and who will be clothed in it if not they alone?

Goodness is for the elect, and who will receive it if not they who have trusted in it from the beginning?

Loving affection is for the elect, and who will be clothed in it if not they who have had it from the beginning?

Walk, all of you, in knowledge of the Most High, and you will know the goodness of the Lord with no holding back from Him, both for His elation and for the fullness of His knowledge.

And His thought has acted as a dispatch, and through it His Will has descended from on high.

And it was sent with the speed of an arrow, shot from a bow with force;
and many hands rushed at the dispatch, to grab it and take it and read it out loud.

Yet it escaped their fingers, and so they were in awe of it and of the seal upon it,
because they did not have the mastery to break open its seal, for the power over the seal was much greater than they.

Even so, those who saw the dispatch ran after it, to find where it would land,

and who would read it out loud, and who would hear it.

Did it not collect upon a cylinder, and spread out over it?
And on it there was the insignia of the Kingdom and the Divine Plan.

And whatever interfered with the cylinder it mowed down and cut to pieces,
and it heaped up a multitude of those who collected against it; and it bridged rivers, filling them with earth,
and passed over and uprooted many forests, and made a wide open way.

From head to foot the dispatch went down, because the cylinder seal rolled out the dispatch to its foot, along with the insignia that was on it.

It was a dispatch of command. And because all regions were included in it,
   there was even visible at its head a head that manifested — even the Son of Truth from the Most High Father.

And so the Son inherited everything and so took possession. And then the scheming of the many ceased:
   All those who lead others astray grew bold at first and then fled; and then those who harass others went limp, and they were blotted out.

And so the dispatch became a great Tablet of the Law that was written entirely by the finger of God.

And so the name of the Father was upon it, and of the Son, and of the Spirit of Holiness, to hold kingly reign for ever and ever.

Hallelujah

ODE 24

A dove fluttered over the head of our Anointed Lord, because He was her head;
　and she chanted over Him, and her voice was heard.

　And nearby residents were awed, and passersby were shaken.
　Flying things gave up taking wing, and every creeping thing died in its hole.

　And primal voids opened and closed, and so screamed out to the Lord as if in labor about to give birth;
　but He was not given to them, to sustain them, because they had no part in Him.

And so the voids were flooded over in the flood of the Lord; and they perished, together with the plan they had remained in from before the beginning;

for they had been in labor from the beginning, and the goal of their labor was the destruction of Life.

And all those who were lacking perished through them, because they could not give the Word so that they might remain.

Thus the Lord put an end to the plans of all those who had no Truth in them.

For they had lacked wisdom, those who exalted themselves in their heart,

*and they were rejected,
because the Truth was not
with them.*

*Because the Lord had
made His Way known, and had
spread His goodness widely,
yet only those who
recognized it knew His
reconciliation.*

Hallelujah

The action begins with the poet already raised up into the Light. As a Son of God, the poet sings of the help God had brought him while he carried on the war of the Word and of the power that God has shown in making the Way smooth, in raising the dead to life, and in preparing the world to be renewed and rebuilt on the rock of Truth for a *habitation of the holy*.

The dragon serpent mentioned in *Ode 22* is one of those anomalous supranatural figures in the Odes, like Shaddai, whose ancient mythology no longer speaks directly to us. The author of the third-century spiritual novel *Pistis Sophia*, who quoted *Ode 22*, saw the seven-headed dragon in this Ode to be one of the Emanations that threatened the upward spiritual progress of the book's heroine, Sophia. Since the discovery of the Odes one hundred years ago, many attempts have been made to identify the seven-headed dragon with one or another more traditional scriptural image. Some point to the dragon serpent's similarity to the seven-headed red sea serpent in the New Testament Book of Revelation, who is at war with heaven and is identified with the devil that empowers Babylon's red beast. Others point to the water snake Leviathan who, according to a passage in the Book of Job, is supposed to lurk in the waters of the Jordan River and whose head was bruised or broken when Jesus was baptized there. Still others equate it with the Lernaean Hydra that Hercules killed as the second of his twelve labors, destroying its poison and searing the roots of its heads.

None of these scriptural comparisons seem very successful, however, because none of them feed the power of the poem. In the image of the seven-headed dragon serpent what I see is a psycho-spiritual reference to the archetypal "subtle body" or "psychic body" composed of the seven major energy centers, each associated with an elemental power or intelligence that corresponds to one of the major nerve plexuses in the physical body. This psychic body is not the immortal spiritual Light body but the body of the Dark nature, a polarized shadow of the true Light nature, which rears its "heads" early in the process of spiritual transformation and must be dealt with.

In the Babylonian Talmud (Kiddushin 29b) there is a story of a battle that parallels the battle of the poet to overcome the dragon serpent in Ode 22. A pious visitor stays the night in the spiritual study hall of a famous sage, not knowing that the hall is haunted by a damaging dragon demon. When the dragon appears to the visitor, he prays, and with every bow he makes in pious prayer, giving thanks and praise to God, one of the seven heads of the dragon falls off.

In *Ode 23* the poet turns to the holy congregation to tell them, in the form of a tall tale, the story of how God's Thought descended to Earth — first as a sealed letter, and then as God's Seal impressed upon the face of the Earth, rolled out by the cylinder seal of God, to announce that God has claimed the Earth and bequeathed it to the Son of Truth — and how His Thought would ultimately manifest as *a great Tablet of the Law.*

A note of explanation on my translation is needed before going on. Where the Syriac word for "wheel" appears in the poem, I have translated it as "cylinder" or "cylinder seal." Cylinder seal is the archeological term used today for the type of "wheel" the poem portrays.

In the ancient Middle East, the "cylinder seal" was a cylindrical wheel made of hard gemstone that bore the image of the seal of an important person along with a message that appeared when it was rolled into clay or earth. For thousands of years, the engraved-gem seal had served as humankind's most important mark of identification. Its owner used it to mark his property, and the seal became the personal mark or "signature" of its owner. It was used to sign documents, to seal goods, and to serve as trademarks on objects, and it was fashioned from locally obtained hard gemstones or the highly prized lapis lazuli. Rolled out on wet clay or other impressionable substance, it produced a positive image. In Parthia, cylinder seals like these were still in use into the first century of the common era to identify large items, even while the signet ring came into use to seal letters and smaller items.

The image of the cylinder seal provides a clarity and coherence to the poem and an additional poetic movement: The Word of God that is sent from heaven in the then-contemporary form of a dispatch — a sealed letter — with superlative speed for that time— the speed of an arrow shot from a bow with force — reverts back to a more ancient message form — a message rolled out by a cylinder seal — and later in the poem reverts to an even more ancient form— a Tablet of the Law like that received by Moses. The Tablet of Moses, too, according to tradition, was engraved on blue sapphire or lapis lazuli.

The cylinder seal in this ode is magnificent, rolled out into the Earth with a message for all the planet and with the image of the Son of Truth upon it together with the insignia of divine government. As it rolls, the cylinder lays out the image of the Lord's Seal and His message and the face of His Son upon the Earth so large that the cylinder uproots trees as it rolls across forests and fills rivers with dirt. Here, it seems to me, we have a tall-tale type of image to make a point: God has come to lay out his Seal upon the Earth and to claim it as the inheritance of his Son, the Messiah. The intention of this ode is to make a gigantic impression, something like the American tall tales of Pecos Bill or Paul Bunyan. The image is primitive and naive, but primitive and naive like the paintings of Paul Gauguin or like Jonathan Swift's larger-than-life character Gulliver.

In *Ode 24* the theme of restoration continues. The poet recounts in lyrical fashion the history of cosmic and spiritual events that occurred when the Son of Truth, God's Anointed Lord, came and was recognized. And the poet tells how and why those who were ignorant of the Word had to perish when the Messiah came in the flood of the Lord's Truth.

ACT II: SCENE 2
RECONCILED WITH GOD'S RIGHTEOUSNESS

ODE 25

I was rescued from my chains, and so I made my way to You, O God,
   because You were the right hand of redemption, and so my helper.
   You held back those rising up against me, and they were seen no more.

Because Your presence was with me, which redeemed me through Your goodness,
   I was despised and rejected in the eyes of many; and so in their eyes I fell like lead,
   and yet from You I gained strength, and relief.

You placed a lamp upon me, both on my right side

and my left, so there would be nothing in me that was not Light, and I was covered with the covering of your Spirit.

And You lifted from me my coat of skin, because Your right hand had lifted me up, and made weakness leave me.

And so I became strong in Your Truth, and reconciled with Your righteousness, and so all those who were against me feared me.

And so I became the Lord's by means of the Lord's name; and I was shown to be righteous through His sweet kindness, and His gentle calm is for ever and ever.

Hallelujah

ODE 26

I well up glory to the Lord, because it is to Him that I belong,
   and I will let His holy ode speak out through me again, because my heart is with Him;
   for his kithara is in my hands, and the odes of His gentle calm will not keep quiet.
   I will call out to Him from my whole heart. I will glorify Him and elevate Him from my every limb.

   For from the East and on to the West that is how it is: The glory belongs to Him.
   And from the South and on to the North it is the same:

To Him belongs the praise of thanks.

And from the foothills of high places to their peaks it is the same: The fullness belongs to Him.

Who finds how to compose the odes of the Lord? Or read them out loud?

Or train his soul for Life, so that his soul may be redeemed?

Or in the Most High find repose, so that the Lord may speak again from his mouth?

Who finds how to interpret the wonders of the Lord?

Because, in fact, it is one's interpretation that will be taken away, and yet what one has interpreted will still remain.

It is enough, in fact, to perceive and so be satisfied. Singers, in fact, as they take their place, find calm,
like a river fed by the pouring out of an increasingly growing spring, and flowing out relief to those who seek it.

Hallelujah

ODE 27

*I reached out my hands and
gave reverence to my Lord,
   because my outspread
hands is his insignia,
   and so my reaching out is
the Cross of Uprightness.*

Hallelujah

ODE 28

Like the wings of doves over their nestlings, with the mouths of their nestlings joined to their mouths, like that are the wings of the Spirit over my heart.

My heart laughs and leaps, like a baby that leaps for joy in the womb of its mother.

I had faith because I was at rest, because the One in whom I had faith is faithful.

Blessed is He, blessed also is my head joined with Him.

And the dagger will not part me from Him, nor the sword,
because I made myself ready before my passing away

had come to be, and I was placed on the breast of The One Who Does Not Die.

And The Life That Does Not Die embraced me, and kissed me,
and of that Life is the Spirit that exists within me; and it cannot die because it is Life.

Those who saw me were astonished, because I had been driven off;
and so they supposed I had been devoured, because to them I seemed like one who had perished.
And yet the injustice done to me became what redeemed me.

I was even reproached by them, because there was no spite in me.

Because I had always done good to everyone, I was hated.

And they surrounded me like rabid dogs, those who, not knowing what they are doing, attack their own masters,

because their thoughts are not straight, and so their minds are altered.

But I held water in my right hand, and so with its sweetness I removed their bitterness.

And I did not perish, because I was not their brother; they did not know my origin, in fact, for my birth was not like theirs;

and yet they tried to execute me; and they were not able, because I was ancient beyond remembrance; and so they came up empty when they cast lots against me.

And those who came into existence after me got nothing when they tried to destroy the remembrance of the one who existed before them
   because the purpose of the Most High cannot be overcome, and His heart transcends all wisdom.

Hallelujah

ODE 29

The Lord is my hope. In Him I will not be shamed by confusion:

A glory like His own He has made for me, and a goodness like His own he has given me,

and to a level of compassion like His own He has raised me, and to a magnificence majestic like His own He has elevated me.

And He brought me up from the depths of the abode of the dead, and from the mouth of death He drew me out.

And I humbled my enemies, and He showed me to be righteous through His goodness, for I had faith in the Lord's Anointed One and considered Him to be Lord.

And He made known to me His insignia, and led me by His Light.
And He has given me the staff of His strength, to subdue the schemes of the peoples, and to humble the power of the mighty,
to make war by His spoken Word, and to take victory by his power.

And by His spoken Word the Lord laid low my enemy, and so my enemy was like dust carried off by the wind.
And I gave the glory of honor to the Most High, because He had made great

His servant and the son of His handmaid.

Hallelujah

ODE 30

Fill water for yourselves from the Living Spring of the Lord, because it has been opened for you.

And so come, every one of you who thirsts, and take a drink, and find rest alongside the Lord's Spring,

because it is bright and pure, and so refreshes the soul continually.

More pleasing, in fact, than honey is its water, and the honeycomb of bees does not compare to it,

because it flows out from the Lord's lips, and from the Lord's heart flows its name.

And as it came, it spread with no limit and was not seen; and so until it was offered in their midst, no one knew it for what it was.

They are good, are they not, those who have drunk from it, and found rest in it?

Hallelujah

Now in a state of redemption, the poet tells in *Ode 25* how his own personal reconciliation with God occurred and how he himself was rescued by God.

> *You placed a lamp upon me, both on my right side and my left, so there would be nothing in me that was not Light, and I was covered with the covering of your Spirit.*
>
> *And You lifted from me my coat of skin, . . .*
>
> (ODE 25)

In *Ode 26*, the poet sings of his work as a poet through whom God speaks. Welling up glory to the Lord, he praises God and defines the work of one who sings and interprets God's Odes.

In *Ode 27* the poet explains the meaning of the reverent posture he assumed when he was raised up into the Light in *Ode 21*. His reaching out is God's sign, the Cross of Uprightness, the same posture God's Anointed One took before He Himself was raised up. In this, the poet prefigures the image of the risen Messiah that opens the final poem of the series, *Ode 42*.

The experience of an immortal in the world, one who knows his spiritual origin and is attacked and harassed by those who do not, is the theme of *Ode 28*. The enjambed verse

Blessed is He, blessed
also is my head joined with Him
(ODE 28)

is an expression of the poet's spirit at rest, and it refers again to the joining of the poet with the Lord God as a crown upon his head, the image of divine regeneration and rebirth that opened the series in *Ode 1*.

The experience of God's Anointed One in the world is the model for the universal experiences of persecution which the poet describes in this Ode. The dagger and the sword mentioned in the poem are images of two distinct instruments of death, one personal, the other impersonal. The Syriac word for blade or dagger, *harba*, is the root of the word used in the first and second centuries to identify the radical Jewish assassins who would secrete themselves in large crowds of people to kill individuals whom the group considered direct or indirect collaborators with the occupying Roman forces. Members of the nonviolent messianic Community would likely have seemed suspect to them. The word used for sword, *shapshera*, is from a Persian word that became the generic term for the primary instrument of Roman execution and invasion. Thus the line recalls the messianic Community attacked from all sides.

Toward the end of the poem, the poet makes a beautifully coherent mystical image when he says that those who were harassing him surrounded him *like rabid dogs* but he was able to turn them from their purpose because he held water in his right hand. Fear of water is the symptom of the later stages of infection with rabies. Whoever is infected with rabies has difficulty swallowing and shows panic when presented with liquids to drink because they cannot quench their thirst. In the poem, the Living Waters that the spiritually ill cannot drink strike fear in them.

In the next Ode, the poet expresses his experiences of the Light of God's Spiritual Sun in recognition of the high spiritual state to which God has lifted him.

> *A glory like His own He has made for me, and a goodness like His own he has given me,*
>
> *and to a level of compassion like His own He has raised me, and to a magnificence majestic like His own He has elevated me.*
>
> *And He brought me up from the depths of the abode of the dead, and from the mouth of death He drew me out.*
>
> (ODE 29)

The poet knows that God's goodness or grace, the immortal body of Light, the body of the immortal soul, is God's raiment, and that it can be put on like clothing, and he has learned its purpose. And the poet continues the theme of God's aid to him in spiritual battle when he sings of the help that the Lord Messiah had given him to overthrow his enemies while he made war by God's Word.

The poet then invites the holy congregation to fill water for themselves from the Living Spring of the Lord that is now open to them, a spring that "refreshes the soul continually" and makes those who drink from it "good."

ACT II: SCENE 3
REDEEMED BY GOODNESS

ODE 31

The primal voids from before the time of the Lord had been dissolved, and Darkness had been broken to pieces by His look.
    Error had grown erratic and had wandered off and perished because of Him; and scorn, with nowhere to go, then sank under the Lord's Truth.

The Lord opened His mouth and spoke goodness and joy, and spoke a new hymn of glory to God's name.
    And while the Lord lifted His voice to the Most High, and presented to Him those who had become His Children by His hands,
    His person also was shown to be righteous, because this

is how His Holy Father had made Him:

"Come forward, you who have been made to suffer, and receive joy,
　and so come into the inheritance of your soul through goodness, and take for yourselves The Life That Does Not Die.

　Even though when it was I who stood up, they charged me with a crime — me, who had not been found guilty of any charge —
　and then they divided the goods they had seized from me, though none of it was in their charge.

　But I endured it, and was silent and held my peace, so that I would not be shaken by them.

Instead, I stood firm and was not shaken, like the truly firm stone that is lashed by great overhanging waves and yet endures.

And I took their bitterness out of humility, because I would then be able to redeem my people and inherit it,
and so not make void the assurances that were made to the patriarchs, to whom I was promised to bring redemption to their seed."

Hallelujah

ODE 32

For the good, there is joy from out of their heart, and Light from out of that which inhabits them;

and from out of True Reality, there is the Word, that which is from itself,

because Truth has been made stronger by the Most High's Holy Power, and Truth is for ever and ever.

Hallelujah

ODE 33

Yet again Goodness took off swiftly and left behind The One Who Corrupts, and then descended upon him so that She could get rid of him;

and so he reduced to nothing that which already lay in ruins before him, and so again corrupted all his work.

And then he stood on the summit of a high peak and cried out with a resounding voice, from one end of the Earth to the other,

and so he drew to him all those who obeyed him, and did not seem like someone evil.

Except that the Perfect Virgin was standing there, speaking plainly and calling them together, and saying:

"You children of man, return, and you, their daughters, come,

and leave the ways of The One Who Corrupts, and draw near Me.

Then I will enter into you, and bring you out from destruction, and make you wise in the ways of Truth.

Do not let yourselves be corrupted, and do not let yourselves perish.

Listen to Me and be redeemed. I am proclaiming to you now the Goodness of God.

And by My hands you will be redeemed and be made good. What I am is your judge.

And they who clothe themselves with Me will not be wronged, but will, in the new world, possess what cannot be corrupted.

My Elect walk with Me. And to those who seek Me, I will make known My ways, and entrust them with My name."

Hallelujah

ODE 34

The Way is not hard where the heart is made simple. And there is no suffering inflicted by upright thoughts. And there is no whirlwind in the depth of enlightened thought.

Where loveliness is wrapped around one on all sides, there is in one nothing caused by discord.

What gives form to that which exists below is what is above.

Everything, in fact, comes from above. And so from below comes nothing, except what is imagined to be by those in whom there is no understanding.

Goodness has been revealed for your redemption. Have faith and so live and be redeemed.

Hallelujah

Through the four Odes in the next scene, the poet speaks in the narrative third person. Led by True Realization and in the presence of Goodness, the poet imparts wisdom and tells tales of the spiritual war waged by the spoken Word.

In *Ode 31* the poet takes up again the narrative he began in *Ode 24* on the cosmic events that took place with the coming of the Anointed One and the flooding of the earth with the Lord's Truth. He quotes the words spoken by the Anointed Lord when He presented to God the Father *those who had become His Children by His hands*. The Messiah, speaking, recalls his judgment (perhaps the judgment of Jesus before the Sanhedrin and Pilate is intended) and his need to go through that judgment to fulfill the prophecy and promise of the patriarchs.

In *Ode 32* the poet makes a short lyric statement of what the good have received since God has made the Word stronger. God's Thought, the Word, calls those who are good back, redeeming them from the Earth.

In *Ode 33* we see Goodness in action. The main actor in the story the poet tells is Goodness Herself, come to Earth to denounce the one who corrupts all things and to announce that She has offered herself to the sons and daughters of Earth so that they may be redeemed. Goodness personified is the Perfect Virgin who appears in the fifth verse of the poem. Keep in mind that the term "virgin" was used in the ancient world for female deities generally, and so the use of the term here would not have seemed as unusual then as it does to us now. She is "perfect" because her being is of God.

Ode 34 is a kind of philosophical commentary or rumination on the arrival of Goodness in *Ode 33*. It is a piece of wisdom literature with the same spiritual coloring as the Hermetic literature being written around the same time period. The poet explains to each of the holy, personally, in the second-person singular, the way things are now that Goodness has appeared for the salvation of each of them and how easy the Way can be for those to whom goodness has been revealed.

ACT II: SCENE 4
RAISED UP INTO THE LIGHT OF TRUE REALIZATION

ODE 35

The fine droplets of the sprinkling of the Lord have shaded me with serenity, and so made a cloud of peace rise upwards over my head
  that has guarded over me always, and has been a salvation for me.

All things were shaken up and filled with terror, and so smoke and judgment spouted out from them.
  And yet was I not calm in the ranks of the Lord's Order? And is the Order not more than a shade of protection, and more than a foundation of support?

And I was carried like a child by its mother, and the Order gave me milk, the dew of the Lord;

and I grew up strong, brought up in the Lord's favor, and I found rest in His fullness;

and I reached out my hands in the ascent of my soul, and I aimed myself toward the Most High, and broke loose toward Him.

Hallelujah

ODE 36

Upon me came to rest the Spirit of the Lord, and She raised me up to the heights
and stood me on my feet in the high place of the Lord, to go before His fullness and His glory,
even while I kept up my glorifying praise in the making of His odes.

From the first She brought me forth into the presence of the Lord,
and even though I was still a son of man, I was named a Light, a Son of God.

Even though I was now glorious among the glorious,

and great among the great

— like the greatness of the Most High, in fact, had the Spirit made me, and like His own renewal had He renewed me —

even so, He anointed me from out of His own fullness; and so I became one of those who are close to Him.

And my mouth was opened like a cloud of dew, and so my heart streamed out a stream of righteousness.

And so in this way I drew close in peace, and I was firmly established in the Spirit of the Divine Plan.

Hallelujah

ODE 37

*I reached out my hands
to the Lord, and took up my
chant to the Most High;
and I spoke with the lips of
my heart, and He heard me;
then, when my chant to Him
fell off,
His Word came to me,
which gave me the fruits of my
labors, and gave me calm in
the goodness of the Lord.*

Hallelujah

ODE 38

I made my ascent into the Light of True Reality as if upon a chariot. And True Realization led me and had me come with Her.

And She brought me across deep chasms and fissures, and from sea cliffs and surging waves She saved me.

And so She became for me a haven of salvation, and placed me upon the step of The Life That Does Not Die.

And She went with me and kept me calm and did not let me wander off in deception, because True Realization is what She was and is.

And I risked no danger

since I continued walking with Her, and I was not deceived in anything because I listened to Her.

Deception, in fact, fled from Her, and never met up with Her again, for True Realization held to the Upright Way.

And whatever I did not understand, She showed me — all the numbing drugs of deception, and also the attractions of hoped for sweetness in death,

and the corruption of one who corrupts, while I watched, being adorned, a bride who brings on corruption and a bridegroom who corrupts and is being corrupted.

And I asked True

Realization, "Who are these?" And She said to me: "This is one who seduces and one who is deceived.

And they imitate The Loved One and His Bride, and deceive the world and so corrupt it.

And they invite many to the wedding feast, and give them the wine of their own drunkenness to drink;
and so these many spew out what they know and what they understand, and are made fit for nonsense.

And then they let them out. And they go about while raving mad, and so they are corrupted:

since in them there is no heart, they do not look for it."

And I was made wise, so I would not fall into the hands of seducers. And I was glad for myself because True Realization had gone with me.

And I was in fact truly centered, and so I was revived and redeemed; and my foundations were laid upon the Lord's hand, because it is He who planted me.
For He had set the shoot, and watered it, and made it ready, and pronounced a blessing over it. And its fruits are forever.
It went deep and then shot up and spread out, and so grew full and large.

And the Lord alone was to be praised, for His planting and also for His skill in cultivation,

for His care and also for the blessing pronounced from His lips, for the beautiful planting of His right hand,

and for the success of His planting, and also for the understanding of His mind.

Hallelujah

In the next four Odes, the poet again speaks in the first person, this time on his personal experience in this new condition. From a variety of perspectives, he provides details of his ascent into the Light and into the presence of God. This is the ascent first described in *Ode 21*.

The poet begins by recalling his tranquillity and enrichment in the ranks of the Lord's Order — how he was protected and remained calm in God's Order while everything else around him was *shaken up and filled with terror*. Then he recounts how he reached out his hands and aimed himself *toward the Most High* and broke loose toward Him.

The Syriac word *rssa* indicates a ceremonial sprinkling or lustration. The word *rsisa* that appears in the first verse of *Ode 35* indicates small drops, fine rain, gentle showers, a sprinkling — like those in a ceremonial purification rite still practiced in the Eastern and Western Roman Church using a sprinkler, or aspergillum.

The image of ascent that ends *Ode 35* leads directly into *Ode 36*, and what happened to the poet as he made his ascent is told in *Odes 36–38*.

In *Ode 36*, the Spirit of the Lord is identified as "she" and acts as the poet's guide throughout the Ode. The poet tells how the Spirit of the Lord *came to rest* upon him and stood him before God, and how in God's presence he was named a Light while still in human form and how he was anointed with the Lord's perfection so that he could draw still nearer to the Lord. Here the poet describes the full perfection of ultimate being in the Light of the Spiritual Sun.

> *Upon me came to rest the Spirit of the Lord, and She raised me up to the heights*
> *and stood me on my feet in the high place of the Lord, to go before His fullness and His glory, ...*
> *She brought me forth into the presence of the Lord,*
> *and even though I was still a son of man, I was named a Light, a Son of God.*
>
> *Even though I was now glorious among the glorious, and great among the great . . .*
> *. . . He anointed me from out of His own fullness; and so I became one of those who are close to Him.*
> *. . .*
> *and I was firmly established in the Spirit of the Divine Plan.*
> (ODE 36)

The glorifying praises of the stream of righteousness which the poet in *Ode 36* says he spoke from his heart seem to me to begin with the verses of *Ode 22*, the Ode which the poet sang as he made his ascent to *the habitation of the holy*.

In *Ode 36*, the poet sings about how he was established in the Image of God — *a Light firmly established in the spirit of the Divine Plan*. In *Ode 37*, he makes his approach to the Most High to receive *the fruits of his labors* — the Word — which give him *gentle rest*. The event of *Ode 36* occurred as he continued to sing praises to God. In *Ode 37* the poet reports that he took up his chant until God's Word came to him to give him the fruits of his labors.

In *Ode 38* the poet narrates what happened as Truth led him into the Light of True Reality *as if in a chariot*. He recounts the sights he saw until Truth made him wise, *truly centered, revived and redeemed*, and he tells how he came to inhabit paradise, planted by God in the Land of the Living. When a man or woman becomes a new person, a being of Light, they then begin to look upon the Image that Adam and Eve saw in the Garden. This is the image which the poet in *Ode 15* calls *The Land of God, The Living That Do Not Die* and which he describes in a vision in *Ode 11*. The poet, a spiritual sapling at the opening of the series, grows through God's Light into a spiritual tree and himself becomes one of the inhabitants of the Land of the Living, one like those he had seen in his vision.

In Jewish literature, this chariot is described as fiery, made of crystal, and with wheels like the Sun. And I think it is worth mentioning that the Syriac word that is translated in *Ode 38* as "chariot" — *merkbta* — is only one of many possible words in Syriac that could have been used to indicate a vehicle. Etymologically it is directly related to the Hebrew word *merkabah*, and so suggests ties with the school of merkabah, or chariot, mysticism that centered on visions of ascent to heavenly realms, a school that emerged in the early centuries of the common era around the time the Odes were written.

ACT II: SCENE 5
LIVING THE LIFE THAT DOES NOT DIE

ODE 39

Surging rivers are like the power of the Lord — those who give it no regard are carried away head after,

and so their paths are twisted, and so their crossings swept away,

and their bodies caught, and so their souls are brought to ruin —

more sudden even than flashes of lightning, and faster
— yet those who cross them in faithfulness will not be shaken,

and those who walk in them with no impurity will not be distressed, because the insignia upon them is the Lord Himself, and the insignia is the Way for those who cross over in the name of the Lord.

Put on, therefore, the name of the Most High and know Him, all of you, and then you will cross at no risk, while the rivers give you willing obedience.

The Lord has built a bridge over them with His spoken Word, and walked on them and so crossed them on foot,
  and the trail of His footsteps stands firm upon the waters and has not been destroyed, but is like a crossbeam fitted in Truth.

On one side and the other, waves kept rising up, yet the footsteps of our Anointed Lord stood firm,

and are not blotted out, nor destroyed.

And the Way that is laid out, is it not for those who cross over after Him? And for those who keep to His path in faithfulness, and revere His name?

Hallelujah

ODE 40

Like honey dripping from the honeycomb of bees, and milk flowing from the woman who loves her children, like this also is the marrow of my hope, my God.

Like a spring streaming out its water, like this is my heart streaming out the Lord's praise; and it leaves my lips as hymns of glory.

And my tongue is sweetened with the business of His anthems, and my limbs are filled out with His odes.

And my face laughs with the feeling of His triumphant joy, and my spirit leaps for joy in His affectionate love, and my being is made bright in Him.

And one who fears can trust in Him, and be assured of redemption in Him;
and the profit of redemption is The Life That Does Not Die, and they who receive it are indestructible.

Hallelujah

ODE 41

Let us glorify the Lord with praise, all of us whom He has brought forth into existence, and take up the Truth of His faithfulness,
   and then his children will be acknowledged by Him, because we will sing by means of His affectionate love.

   We live in the Lord by means of His goodness, and we receive life by means of His Anointed One. The Great Day indeed has shone upon us!

   And since He is wonderful, He who has given to us from His own glories, let us be equal in concord because of this, all together in the name of the Lord, and so let us honor Him in His goodness.

And let our faces shine by means of His Light, and let our hearts meditate on His affectionate love.
By night and by day, let us leap for joy in the joyous dance of the Lord.

And let all those who see me be astonished, because I am descended from the race of a different father,
for I have been remembered by the Father of Truth — He the One I belonged to from the beginning —
for His rich abundance has brought me into existence, and the thought of His heart.

And with us along our Way is His spoken Word, the Redeemer who gives Life and does not reject our souls,

   the strong man who was brought low, and yet was raised high by His own righteousness.

The Son of the Most High has appeared, the perfect fullness of His Father,

   and Light dawned from the spoken Word, which was in Him before the beginning.

In truth He is the Anointed One, and He was acknowledged before the laying of the foundations of the world,

   so that He could give Life to souls forever by the Truth

of His name — a new glory for the Lord from those who are deeply attached to Him.

Hallelujah

ODE 42

"I reached out My hands and came nearer to My Lord, because My outspread hands is His insignia,

and so both My own reaching out and the simple form of the Cross, which was raised up, suspended on the Way of Uprightness.

And since then I have been of no use to those who did not know Me, because I will be hidden from those who did not take hold of Me,

and so I will be only with those who love Me deeply.

All those who have harassed Me have died. And yet those who looked for Me waited for Me, because I am Living;

and I arose in them, and I am with them, and I will speak through their mouths.

Did they not, in fact, rid themselves of those who harass them? And over them I threw the yoke of My loving affection.

Like the arm of a bridegroom over a bride, like this is My yoke over those who know Me;

and like the nuptial tent stretched out in the home of a bridal pair, like this is My loving affection over those who trust in Me.

I was not really gotten rid of, though I seemed to be, and

I did not really perish, though they thought it of Me.

The abode of the dead caught sight of Me and groaned, and Death spewed Me out and many with Me.

Like vinegar or some bitter thing I became to him, and I went down within Death to his deepest depth;

and then he went limp, both feet and head, because he could not bear My presence there.

And I made a congregation of the Living among his dead, and I spoke to them with living lips, because then My Word would not fail.

And then those who had died ran toward Me. And then

they cried out and said: 'Son of God, have compassion for us,

and so treat us with Your kindness, and lead us out from the bondage of Darkness.

And open for us the door that comes out to You, for we can see that You are not touched by our death.

Allied with You, even we can be redeemed, because You are our redeemer.'

I heard their voice, and put their faithfulness in My heart,

and put My name upon their head, because they are freeborn, they are noble, and they are Mine."

Hallelujah

The last scene of the entire dramatic sequence, played out in the final four Odes, shows what Living The Life That Does Not Die is all about.

In *Ode 39*, the poet lays out a narrative on the Way that the Lord Messiah had established since His victory had been won. The poet uses the image of the Messiah's footsteps as a crossbeam set across surging rivers, which are like the Lord's power, and he calls out a reminder to the holy that the Way set by the Messiah is laid out for those who cross after Him in his name.

Ode 40 addresses God but speaks about the poet's hope in the Lord Messiah. The imagery emphasizes it. The first line compares his hope to honey and milk and marrow—all special foods. The third line speaks of the poet's tongue, the organ of taste, being sweetened, and of the poet's limbs being filled out, as if he had been fed on milk. The mention of marrow, for centuries used figuratively to represent bodily strength, makes of the poet's hope the bones that have held him straight and firm. The poet streams out praise of the Lord Messiah and reminds the holy that those who trust in Him can be assured of redemption, and that the profit of redemption is The Life That Does Not Die. And the value of redemption is clear.

> ... *the profit of redemption is The Life That Does Not Die, and they who receive it are indestructible.*
> (ODE 40)

The grande finale begins with *Ode 41*. This poem is a grand conclusion of praise to the Lord God, the Father of Truth, because the Great Day is come and the Anointed One has appeared and is with them. The poet calls on the congregation of the redeemed to glorify the Lord God with praise so that He will recognize them as His Children.

Because the Great Day now shines upon them, they all live in the Lord God and *receive Life* by means of His Anointed One, and the poet sings in joy at the fact that God, the Father of Truth, has acknowledged him as His Son. The poet closes the Ode with the acknowledgment of the Redeemer, the Son of the Most High, who had appeared in order to help them and to give Life to their souls by his Truth.

In the final Ode in the series and the grand finale, *Ode 42*, the poet recounts the last stage of the Messiah's work in the Messiah's own words. The resurrected Son of the Most High sings of His earthly destiny and His ministry, a ministry which continues with those in whom He has arisen. The spoken words of the resurrected Anointed One end the song with the story of how He defeated death and claimed as His own a congregation of the Living from among the dead.

The beautifully intricate opening of this Ode, a variation and extension of *Ode 27*, depicts the moment of the Messiah's passing, His hands spread out on the cross of His crucifixion. His outspread arms, He says, form the *simple form* of God's insignia, the Cross that was suspended on the Way of Uprightness: the cosmic Cross of

Uprightness. The Cross of Uprightness is first mentioned in *Ode 27*. It is mentioned again and raised to cosmic proportions in *Ode 42*.

In ancient Syriac there was no word that had the primary meaning of "cross" in the sense of an archetypal symbol or insignia. But there was the word *qaysa*, which appears in the Odes to signify the archetypal Cross. The primary meaning of this word is "wood," "a piece of wood," or "a wooden vessel," and its secondary meanings are "a stick," "a tree," and "a cross." There is another Syriac word for cross, but that word is never used in the Odes. That word relates directly to crucifixion and the cross of the crucifixion, an ignoble meaning which the poet of the Odes, I am sure, purposely avoided when he attempted to evoke the archetypal symbol of the cosmic Cross or Seal of God.

The section of the second-century text the Acts of John called "Revelation of the Mystery of the Cross" sheds some light on this archetypal image. This section of the Acts records a message reportedly revealed to the disciple John upon the Mount of Olives through the Image of Jesus while the man Jesus was being tormented and crucified nearby on Golgotha:

> He showed me a Cross of Light firmly fixed, and around the Cross a great crowd, which had no single form; and in the Cross was one form and the same likeness.
>
> And I saw the Lord himself above the Cross, having no shape but only a kind of voice; yet not

that voice which we knew, but one that was sweet and gentle and truly the voice of God, which said to me, "John, there must be one man to hear these things from me; for I need one who is ready to hear.

"This Cross of Light is sometimes called Logos by me for your sakes, sometimes mind, sometimes Jesus, sometimes Christ, sometimes a door, sometimes a way, sometimes bread, sometimes seed, sometimes resurrection, sometimes Son, sometimes Father, sometimes Spirit, sometimes life, sometimes truth, sometimes faith, sometimes grace; and so it is called for men's sake.

"But what it truly is, as known in itself and spoken to us, is this: it is the distinction of all things, and the strong uplifting of what is firmly fixed out of what is unstable, and the harmony of wisdom, being wisdom in harmony.

"But there are places on the right and on the left, powers, authorities, principalities and demons, activities, threatenings, passions, devils, Satan and the inferior root from which the nature of transient things proceeded.

"This Cross then is that which has united all things by the Word and which has separated off what is transitory and inferior, which has also compacted all things into one.

"But this is not that wooden Cross which you shall see when you go down from here; nor am I the man who is on the Cross, I whom now you do not see but only hear my voice.

"I was taken to be what I am not, I who am not what for many others I was; but what they will say of me is mean and unworthy of me.

"Since then the place of rest is neither to be seen nor told, much more shall I, the Lord of this place, be neither seen nor told.

"The multitude around the Cross that is not of one form is the inferior nature.

"And those whom you saw in the Cross, even if they have not yet one form — not every member of him who has come down has yet been gathered together.

"But when human nature is taken up, and the race that comes to me and obeys my voice, then he who now hears me shall be united with this race and shall no longer be what he now is, but shall be above them as I am now.

"For so long as you do not call yourself mine, I am not what I am; but if you hear me, you also as hearer shall be as I am, and I shall be what I was, when you are as I am with myself; for from me you are what I am.

"Therefore ignore the many and despise those who are outside the mystery; for you must know that I am wholly with the Father, and the Father with me."

Acts of John, trans. M. R. James
(Oxford: Clarendon Press, 1924)

Speaking in the voice of John, the author of these Acts closes the section with these words:

I held this one thing fast in my mind, that the Lord had performed everything as a symbol and a dispensation for the conversion and salvation of man.

The information preserved in the Acts of John tells us that this form of the Cross signifies not the wooden cross of crucifixion but the Cross of Light.

The exploits of the Apostle Thomas, who is considered the first Apostle of the ancient messianic Church of the East and its founder, are described in the fourth-century Syrian document known as the Acts of Thomas. Its version of history records that the Apostle Thomas traveled to India, then to China, and later returned to India, where he was put to death by a mob incited by Brahmin priests. The image of the archetypal Cross is engraved on the tomb of Thomas at Mylapore in the south of India near Madras (now Chennai). The same image appears in a number of other churches in southern India.

Saint Thomas Cross

This image of the Cross of Light also appears at the head of an eighth-century document carved into stone in China. In the year 781 CE, a monument was erected in the western suburb of the Chinese capital at Ch'ang-an to commemorate the mission of the ancient Church of the East to the great T'ang dynasty. The stone is known in Chinese as *ching-chiao pei*, which may be translated as "Monument of the Teaching of Light" or "Monument of the Great-Sun Religion."

The nominal purpose of the monument was to praise the emperors under whom the East Asian Church had flourished in China. The verses of an ode and a long prose preface to the ode in Chinese occupy the stone's face. The preface opens with an outline of the doctrines of the Teaching and the practices of its ministers. A transition paragraph relates the difficulties of naming the true, unchanging System but tells that the name finally settled upon is the "Teaching of Light" before the doctrinal portion of the inscription turns into historical narrative.

The symbols cut into the crown of the stone form a figurehead design. An immense pearl is held between two monstrous creatures with the bodies of fish coiled into the shape of snakes, a design common among Buddhists of the time. According to the Pure Land Sastra, the pearl signifies the Law of Buddha. In the center of the headpiece, beneath the pearl and framed on either side by sprigs of either myrtle or lily (either a Buddhist or Christian emblem), is the apex of a triangle that forms a canopy over a significant incised scene: The Flying Cloud of Chinese Muslims and Taoists rising out of the Buddhist Lotus Flower to support the Cross of the Apostle Thomas, which is ignited from above.

Cross and Figurehead from the Eighth-century
Chinese Monument of the Teaching of Light

The descendants of the ancient Church of the East, still in existence today but split and factioned, retain the same form of the Cross as their sign:

Cross of the Present-day Church of the East

The image of this Cross has been carried into our own time in silhouette also as the Cross of the Eastern Orthodox Church:

Contemporary Eastern Orthodox Cross

With rectified proportions and symmetry, the image of this same Cross was revealed in our own time to the Second Advent Church, whose members know it also as the Great Seal of Christ, the sign of God's Image and Word in the Spiritual Sun of Righteousness:

Second Advent Solar Cross
or Great Seal of Christ

Epilogue

THE ODES OF SOLOMON CELEBRATE the communion with the Image and Word, the pregnant spiritual phase that was offered in the time of Jesus and that was terminated a few generations later by the powers of the world. The Odes represent the ancient version of this hoped-for time, the Great Day of God, the new Age of the Living, the age when God makes His Second Advent. This is the communion being offered again in our time.

This ultimate potential represents for us God's Second Advent Appearance, the Presence of God, which can be experienced only by spiritual faculties. As the Odes depict, these faculties need to be reborn, regenerated, and given life. And this process of renewal is the work of God's Image. Within this Image is a mediating force, a spiritual Seed, and this force gives Life. Through it we are reborn in spirit. We take on again a spiritual Light Body, which is immortal, and we are given a spiritual Consciousness by which to process God's Word.

The spiritual Light Body, nonphysical and nonpsychic, lives on Divine Intelligence and Energy. It kills nothing. It lives on nothing except God's Love, Truth, Wisdom, Knowledge, and Righteousness. Imagine such a being capable of living upon nothing but God's Light, God's Divine Presence, never knowing suffering and never knowing death. Imagine a number of such beings gathered together in a Community of the Living, a new Community of Light on Earth. This is the image to be fulfilled in our age.

Remarks On The Life And Times Of The Odes Of Solomon As Conclusion

It is no surprise that written copies of the Odes, both in Syriac and in Greek, more or less disappeared from the world of history. By the beginning of the fourth century, Latin had replaced Greek throughout the western Mediterranean and Greek-speaking copyists had no incentive to continue copying Greek scriptural manuscripts. From that time forward, whatever did not appeal to the tastes of Latin-speaking copyists simply ceased to exist. But there was another component to this new international pattern: The literature of the Living tradition began to be transmitted in the spoken languages of various peoples—Egyptian, Syrian, Aramaic— and in a short time, the scriptures of the Living grew into provincial spiritual literatures. Eventually, through carelessness and catastrophe, these literatures too were lost, the Odes of Solomon among them. And it was during the Latin century that the Odes made their final appearances in the ancient Western world. History down to our own time has proceeded without them, and without the knowledge of the spiritual experience they express. Three records of their existence remain to us. This note will provide an account of each of them and of their circumstances.

A Citation of Lactantius the Rhetorician

The Latin rhetorician Lactantius (240–320 CE) quoted a line from the Odes (which we now know to be from the 19th Ode) in his major work, *Divine Institutes* (Book IV.12). Lactantius, a new convert to Roman Christianity at the time he wrote his book, and unfamiliar with its scriptures, believed, erroneously, that his citation was a genuine prophecy of King Solomon that would provide divine support for his argument in favor of the doctrine of the Virgin Birth. (Scholars suppose he did not take the line directly from a collection of the Odes but from an excerpt of them he had found in a second-century book of testimonies of the kind compiled by Justin Martyr.) Lactantius published the first edition of his work sometime between 303 and 311. The circumstances in which he was writing may have caused the haste that contributed to his error.

At the beginning of the Latin century, the considerable reputation of Lactantius won him an imperial appointment to a prime teaching position at the imperial court of Nicomedia in the province of Bithynia on the Anatolian Peninsula. His appointment was part of the plan of the aging emperor Diocletian to transform the Greek city of Nicomedia into a new Latin capital in the Greek East. To add to the splendor of his imperial court, the emperor also summoned other notables. One was a renowned philosopher (whom Lactantius does not name but whom he chides in his writings), an old-school teacher of poverty and abstinence and the author of three books against Christians. Another was the regional governor Sossianus Hierocles, a strong campaigner at court against Christians and soon to be an avid enforcer of the edicts against them in Bithynia and Egypt. Also summoned were the two young caesars of Diocletian's newly devised ruling tetrarchy: Galerius, Diocletian's adopted imperial heir, the natural son of a Thracian herdsman and a Dacian mother, and Constantine, the heir presumptive of his own natural father, Constantius.

These two imperial heirs, in the near future, would become imperial opponents, one of them the champion of Lactantius. Galerius, in the next months, would instigate imperial edicts against Christians and enforce them ferociously for a decade in the eastern empire, until he was near death. (Galerius's unspoken dream was to make Rome a Dacian empire, and to impose on Rome's citizens the cruelty of the conqueror on the conquered in retribution for the treatment his Dacian ancestors had received at the hands of Trajan two hundred years before.) Constantine, who would come to rule after him, after twenty divisive years of civil war, would declare himself sole emperor of Rome and declare that Rome be an empire of Roman Christian orthodoxy.

All of this collection of imperial courtiers became Lactantius's acquaintances, if not his familiars, during the many months he remained in Nicomedia. All but Constantine became the anonymous rhetorical opponents Lactantius dialogued with in the seven books of his *Divine Institutes*. Most became tragic characters in his treatise *On the Deaths of the Persecutors*, a history framed by the succession of their tortured and (to him) providential deaths.

In the tensions that preceded the publication of Galerius's First Edict against Christians (303), Lactantius resigned his post but remained in the city for a time, long enough to be able to report firsthand on the February day when soldiers ransacked the main church in the center of Nicomedia while he was teaching the culture of oratory down the street. And long enough to record the odious effects of the Second Edict a few days later: the beheading of the city's bishop and the burning and drowning of other Christians. By May, Diocletian had abdicated and retired to a distant palace on the Dalmatian coast — famously, to grow cabbages. Lactantius, too, retired. We do not know where, but somewhere outside the reach of Galerius, he completed and published the *Divine Institutes*, an apology for Roman Christian philosophy in response to Sossianus Hierocles's two-volume critique of the Bible. Throughout the ten years of persecution Lactantius lived in poverty. Then Constantine emerged victorious and, two years later, the emperor became Lactantius's patron. Lactantius, for the few years of life remaining to him, served as tutor to Constantine's son and counselor to the emperor on religious policies, advocating the marriage of the

Roman Christian faith with the Roman wisdom tradition.

When Constantine entered Rome victorious in 312, he neglected to perform the customary sacrifice at the Temple of Jupiter but honored the Senate with a visit, which in turn honored him with the title Great Augustus. Immediately after the armed conflicts that followed the end of the persecutions, Constantine offered to Romans, in the so-called Edict of Milan (313), "freedom to follow whatever religion each one wished" in order that "whatever divinity there is in the seat of heaven may show to Rome His accustomed favor and benevolence." Sol Invictus replaced Mars on Constantine's coinage, and the emperor himself instructed Christians and non-Christians alike to unite in observing the Venerable Day of the Sun.

After Lactantius's death, Constantine retracted his original offer of religious freedom and instead initiated reprisals — beheadings and book burnings — against those who did not conform to the doctrines of the growing new orthodoxy. In 325 he called the famous Council of Nicaea to declare, once and for all, throughout the empire, what was acceptable to teach regarding the nature of Christ. At that exclusive convention, sponsored by the emperor, a few hundred bishops endorsed not the System of Spiritual Transformation taught and practiced by their Lord but a homogenized creed and an anathema; that is, they professed confident belief in an untestable spiritual theory and a condemnation of all those who did not profess it. Constantine enforced the break with Jewish tradition agreed upon in the Council of Nicaea by prohibiting the celebration of the Lord's Supper on 14 Nisan, the day before Jewish Passover.

Constantine dedicated his new capital of Constantinople in 330 adorned in the sun-rayed diadem of Apollo; and for the next several years he increased the minting of coins while he confiscated and melted down all the gold, silver, and bronze statues from the old Roman temples (which he had declared imperial property) except for a number of bronzes he selected to be public monuments to adorn the new capital.

Later in his rule, Constantine showed a new disdain for the "barbarians" beyond the frontiers of Rome. In 336 he rebuilt Trajan's Bridge across the Danube and reconquered Dacia from the Goths, taking the title *Dacicus Maximus*. In his final year, he made plans for a Christian crusade against Persia. In a letter to Shapur II, the shah of Persia, Constantine asserted his patronage over Persia's Christian subjects and urged Shapur to treat them well. Then he called for bishops to accompany him and commissioned a tent in the shape of a church to follow him and his army. Constantine had planned to be baptized in the Jordan River before he crossed into Persia, but in the spring of 337 he called off the campaign when he fell ill. He received baptism just before he died in the suburbs of Nicomedia on his way back to the resting place he had secretly prepared for himself in Constantinople.

Whether Constantine's words to Shapur were sincere or were intended to provoke reprisals against the Eastern Christian population, the shah did react. Soon after Constantine's death, Shapur, perhaps feeling the threat of Christians in his realm as well as an impending Roman invasion, broke the forty-year peace with Rome and began a long and successful campaign against Constantine's successors, including an invasion of Mesopotamia and the Roman client kingdom of Armenia. And then, in imitation of the Roman orthodoxy Constantine had instituted, Shapur established his own Persian orthodoxy. The shah ordered the codification of the Zoroastrian scriptures, the Avesta, and enforced doctrinal unity: All Zoroastrian sects that did not abide by his new orthodoxy were called false and heretical and were persecuted along with the Christians.

The Parodies of Ephrem the Syrian

Half a century after Lactantius, Ephrem of Syria (306–373 CE), writing as a Roman theologian, quoted the Odes of Solomon to malign their tenets. Ephrem was born and raised in the Roman fortress city of Nisibis in Mesopotamia, and there he learned the Roman concepts of Christ from the bishop of the city, a signatory at the Council of Nicea in 325. When Persia again attacked the eastern regions of Rome in 359, the cities around Nisibis fell one by one, their citizens killed or deported. In 363 the Roman emperor Julian advanced to the Sassanian capital at Ctesiphon but could not take the city. During his retreat, Julian was mortally wounded by a Sassanian spearman and died in his tent. Julian's successor, Jovian, was unable to respond. To save Rome's army, Jovian surrendered the city of Nisibis and permitted the expulsion of its entire Christian population.

Ephrem joined that Christian exodus westward and settled in Edessa. There he was at the heart of the Syriac-speaking world, in a city whose inhabitants identified it with the biblical Ur of the Chaldees, the traditional birthplace of the patriarch Abraham. The city, cultivated and Roman in dress but Parthian and Armenian in flavor, was surrounded by desert and full of rival philosophies and religions. Urbane Christians, Neoplatonists, and Jews lived in close contact. Nicene Christians there were called "Palutians," named by the city's inhabitants for a former Roman bishop of Edessa, with the same disdain that Nicene Christians had named other messianic communities whose teachings did not conform to the dictates of the Nicene Council either "Arians," "Marcionites," "Manichees," or "Bardaisanites" after their respective spiritual theorists and founders (and with the same disdain that later Roman Nicene Christians would call nonconforming Germanic Nicenes "Lutherans" and "Protestants" and would by them be called "Papists").

The emperor Julian, a nephew of Constantine, had promoted religious freedom and had revered the Unconquerable Sun. But he had also promoted the awful state theurgy of blood sacrifice, following the prescription of the Neoplatonist philosopher Iamblichus (in opposition to his more spiritual teacher, Plotinus), an outmoded practice which the emperor was trying to bring back into vogue. It was after Julian's death, and after Ephrem's own exile, that Ephrem was taken up by the Nicene movement to become the enemy to all that was unlike itself. He created disagreeable and mediocre mutations of the Odes of Solomon to make them conform to his Roman orthodoxy and then used those verses to power his own propaganda hymns to make lyrical attacks against the teachings of the city's revered and long dead teacher Bardaisan (154–222). The word play of Ephrem's verses indicate that both Ephrem the parodist and Bardaisan the teacher had known the Odes in Syriac, and in much the same form as they have come down to us.

The ascetic Ephrem called the genteel and saintly Bardaisan "the philosopher of Aramaeans," to associate him with the Syrian gnostics of the centuries that preceded him, and "the teacher of Mani," to associate him with the famous third-century gnostic that followed him. For nearly two hundred years, the Odes had been employed at the Mystery School of Bardaisan to teach a Living Spiritual System. This System, like the Odes, interpreted the physical body to be a "coat of skin" which the soul had to shed, and referred to the God of All as "Father of the Living," and taught the resurrection of the spiritual body of Light and not the mortal body. Bardaisan's School, outside of Roman control during the two hundred years of its existence, had maintained its association with Jewish teachings, in addition to the New Covenant writings, long after it was fashionable — or possible — to do so in Rome. During these centuries, Bardaisan's spiritual hymns had lived on the lips of Edessans like folk songs, until Ephrem mimicked their meter and melodies in parody and, to enhance their popular appeal, rehearsed all-women choirs of young virgins to sing them in the city forums.

Bardaisan, the greatest psalmist of the second century, had written, like King David, 150 hymns according to Ephrem. A talented poet,

Bardaisan had been raised in wealth at the court of King Abgar VIII in Edessa and had shared the education and friendship of the crown prince. In the account of Bardaisan's life by Michael the Syrian, the young poet-scholar had been initiated into the Mysteries of Christ at the age of twenty-five by Bishop Hystaspes, whom he had happened to hear speak in Edessa, and after a time he was ordained. Already compendious in his knowledge, Bardaisan, now ordained to teach, founded a spiritual community that soon replaced the Marcionites as the chief Christian group in and around Edessa.

By the end of the twentieth year of Abgar's reign (197 CE), the Roman emperor Septimus Severus had created the province of Osrhoene around the city of Edessa and put its administration in charge of a Roman procurator, the latest political move in the region by Rome against its opponent Persia. Abgar was left with only the city of Edessa as his kingdom. Until the end of his reign, the coinage of Abgar's realm read "Lucius Aelius Aurelius Septimus Abgar." (This Abgar is sometimes credited with being the first Christian king, but according to Persian sources he had been a convert to Judaism like his father and not to Christianity.)

After the death of the old king Abgar in 212, his son the crown prince became ruler of the small kingdom of Edessa as Abgar IX. For two years Bardaisan worked with his royal friend, in ways unknown to us, to establish Edessa as the first kingdom of the Living, until an anti-Christian faction in the city-kingdom conspired with the new Roman emperor, Caracalla, the eldest son of Septimus Severus, to overthrow the young king. Abgar was captured, deposed, and sent in chains to Rome, summoned there by the new emperor to be murdered. Bardaisan, against the advice of Caracalla's cronies, refused to denounce his own doctrines. Then in 217, in an act of personal retribution by one of his bodyguards, Caracalla himself was murdered while he was urinating on the roadside just outside the city gates of Edessa, on his way to tour the famous Moon Temple at Harran. Bardaisan took the opportunity to flee eastward and took refuge in the Castle of Oblivion in Kuzestan (known in Armenian sources as the Fortress of Ani). There, in the few years that remained to him, he read the temple record and the chronicle of kings and added to it the events of his own day. The history of Moses of Chorene recounts that Bardaisan wrote his chronicle book in Syriac and that it was soon afterward translated into Greek.

The Teachings of *Pistis Sophia*

In Upper Egypt, during the third and fourth centuries, there was an attempt to resurrect the message of the Odes again, in a collection of writings known today as the *Pistis Sophia* (a subscript in the text identifies it by the more suitable title *A Selection from the Books of the Savior*). The ancient editors of this voluminous miscellany tell us that they had selected the pieces that appear under this title from a fuller collection, and tell us also that they have omitted in their selection the higher mysteries. Today, however, even these pieces are apocryphal in the original sense of the word: reserved for the initiated. Throughout the collection there is presupposed a highly complex system of aeons, represented as a system of stages, each of which, at earlier times in spiritual history, had been the summit of transcendental teaching in its time. In the collection, these progressive revelations are subordinated one to another in succession and superseded by the teachings of the New Covenant. In this way, the entire wisdom tradition of the ancients had been preserved.

The mysteries in the book are closely entwined with the lore of the glory of the Light body. Jesus, whose ministry is not only earthly but cosmic and supercosmic, is everywhere, preeminent and central. Yet nowhere does the Greek term *Christ* appear, and nowhere is there a sign of antagonism to Judaism or the Jewish Testament. The text that became the modern namesake of the collection is the famous spiritual *bildungsroman* whose heroine is Sophia, a Light Being lost in the aeons of chaos in the process of being saved. It is in this novel tale, the *Pistis Sophia*, that the Odes are quoted. While Jesus sits with his disciples, male and female, on the Mount of Olives in the twelfth year of his Resurrection, he describes the salvation of Sophia as she rises out of the higher regions of chaos. Between chapters 58 and 71, excerpts of five of the Odes of Solomon (Odes 1, 5, 6, 22, 23) are quoted by the disciples of Jesus, along with a few verses of David's Psalms, as solutions to the riddles of misfortune and penitence that Sophia expounds upon in the modern Gnostic language of the day as she makes her way up to more spiritual realms.

*

In Rome, Lactantius's systematic presentation of Roman Christian thought came to be considered somewhat heretical after his death. In the sands of Egypt, the manuscript of *Pistis Sophia*, like the codices of the Nag Hammadi library, was hidden, probably before 350, when "heretics" in Roman Christian congregations and their writings were being hunted down throughout the empire and expunged. In 373, Ephrem, after a ten-year residency in Edessa, succumbed to a plague whose victims he had ministered to. Another century goes by, with its vicissitudes and agonies and mutations. Bardaisan's Teachings gradually appear more heretical. By 380 a popular orthodoxy becomes the official state religion of Rome under Theodosius I. Around 400 the schools and liturgical centers of the Marcionites and the Bardaisanites in Edessa are destroyed by a Bishop Rabbula and replaced with a church of Nicene orthodoxy, and the message of the Odes is buried. Ephrem's hymns grow in popularity — Nicene Christian poets write hundreds of pseudepigraphical works in his name for the next eight centuries. Yet for the remainder of time, Bardaisan's own works are known only through secondhand accounts, primarily in Syriac, and most notably in the writings of his antithesis, Ephrem. The Living continue to flee through the centuries along the Silk Road, always to the East, establishing refugee colonies and monastic communities wherever they are welcomed for a time — in Sassanid Persia, in Persia's far-eastern province of Khorasan, and in China. And over these centuries, the secret of the Living is hidden with them. Eventually, with them, the secret leaves the world.

The learned Anglican theologian William Whiston, successor to his mentor Isaac Newton in the chair of mathematics at Cambridge, and notorious in his anti-Nicene heterodoxy, was the first to notice a line of the Odes in the writings of Lactantius; he had been searching through ancient records for evidence of true Living Ones in the age before the Nicene pogrom for his 1728 opus *A Collection of Authentick Records Belonging to the Old and New Testament* (col. 1, 155). The books and hymns of Ephrem have continued to be known throughout the Western world without interruption for 1700 years, and they carry with them wisps of the memory of Bardaisan. In the eighteenth century the apocryphal anthology known as the *Pistis Sophia* was raised from its dry grave in Egypt to the shelves of the British Museum and perused there by readers for thirty years before one of them, a Danish bishop, recognized the verses of five of the Odes of Solomon embedded in its teaching targums. In 1909 J. Rendel Harris, an appreciative scholar of ancient Syriac scripture, found a more or less complete collection of the messianic Odes among a heap of manuscripts he had purchased "somewhere in Mesopotamia," and he translated them into sonorous English. Since that time, others have retranslated and interpreted and misinterpreted them, and have attempted to identify their author and their place of origin. My pages simply attempt to aerate the small field of known events that surround the hiding places from which the Odes have been secreted into the future for us.

Two Afterwords

Three Poets on Translating Poetry

KENNETH REXROTH: "The Poet as Translator" (1961)

IN THE 1960S THE AMERICAN poet Kenneth Rexroth attempted to illustrate the theory of "sympathetic translation" developed by the seventeenth-century English poet John Dryden. Rexroth, in his essay, provides a summary explanation of the process and an exemplary exhibition of successful translations from a variety of languages into twentieth-century American English. The theory holds that the translation of poetry into poetry is the act of identifying oneself with another person, the actual transmutation of the other's utterance into one's own utterance. For Rexroth, the ideal translator is an all-out advocate, and the act of identification is so complete that the translator speaks with the veridical force of his own utterance while he remains conscious of communicating the other directly to his own audience. Thus Rexroth conveys what he thinks the poet does in the living relationship of translation, in the actual act.

All successful translations exemplify this very high degree of imaginative identification with their originals. And the prime criterion of successful poetic translation is assimilability.

Communion is as important to the poet-translator as communication. (Rexroth points out that all the greatest translators of Chinese in his time knew less than nothing of Chinese when they did their best translations.) Sympathy, he says, can carry you very far if you have the talent to go with it. Sympathy, or at least projection, can also carry you *too* far. And that is the danger.

ROBERT BLY: *The Eight Stages of Translation* (1986)

Of the next generation of poet translators after Rexroth, one, Robert Bly, developed a demonstrable method of translation that lessens the danger of "being carried too far." He described the method in the book-length essay *The Eight Stages of Translation* (1986). In this essay he does not deal with the theory of translation but, like Rexroth, tries to answer the question, What is it like to translate a poem? And Bly demonstrates his answer by going step-by-step through the process using a short poem in German that he did not know very well.

He looks mainly at the difficulties—the difficulties that are really all one difficulty: "something immense, knotted, exasperating, fond of disguises, resistant, confusing, all of a piece." A poem is translated in fits and starts, a half line here, later the other half, but there is a process. Bly simplifies the process into eight stages that the translator goes through from the first meeting with a poem to the time of its re-creation, when one says good-bye to it. Often these stages collapse into each other. At other times a single line will go through all eight stages in a flash while the other lines around it lie about looking even more resistant than before. What we do then is pretend that all goes in order, just as we do when we make a map: we pretend the earth can be laid out flat. But the map helps us to visualize the territory. I set out Bly's eight stages as follows:

1

During the first stage we set down a literal version without worrying about nuances. English phrases that are flat, prosaic, or dumpy are fine; we only want the thrust. With the literal, the poem itself disappears. What is missing is probably the meaning.

2

To find what the poem *means* is what Bly calls the second stage. Some translators just print the literal version and turn away from this stage. If we enter this stage, we will need everything we have learned and everything we can scrape together about the original language to penetrate the problems. During this stage a native-born speaker is helpful to settle the ambiguous meanings a dictionary will not and so shorten the time we spend floundering, trying to ascertain whether the primary or secondary meaning of a term is the one being used in the poem.

When a poet from another culture contradicts our assumptions—that is, does not support our own prejudices—we tend to deal with his point in a vague and inadequate way that tends to conceal it or mislead the reader; for this reason it is extremely important to struggle with each eccentricity we see.

As we work, we find ourselves drawn into areas we do not feel confident in, even to ideas we cannot accept. But if we cannot accept them, we will resist them as a translator and do a poor job translating the poem.

During this stage, then, we test how far we are willing to go. So we need to estimate how much resistance we have, or we need to inwardly sense whether we believe what the poet is saying though it may contradict most of our cultural assumptions. If we do not believe it, we should let the poem alone and not translate it; we will just ruin it if we go ahead.

We have to sense, or else figure out, what each word is doing in the poem; otherwise, the poem will not be clear. There is enough ambiguity produced by the forced movement from one language to another; we do not need to add to the uncertainty by having trust in "poetic ambiguity," which amounts to refusing to think the question through or risk an answer. We adopt solutions. Those solutions may of course be wrong, but adopting solutions allows us to put the details together into a meaningful whole for the first time. And we may end up with quite a different meaning than we arrive at by reading the literal version.

In a good poem that violates certain unspoken cultural or intellectual assumptions, the second stage may take several hours. When working with a complicated poem, the translator can easily get pulled into a bypath for a time, but none of that time is wasted. The more one talks, the clearer the original poet's beliefs become, and thus so does his meaning.

But if the store of feeling in a poem is beyond the translator, he should let the poem be. At the end of this stage, the translator should ask himself whether the feelings as well as the concepts are within his world. If they are not, he should stop. These feelings can't be faked.

Thus it is that in the second stage we decide whether to turn back or go on.

3

If we decide to go on, we return to our literal version to see where the literal version lost the meanings we just found. We redo the literal and try to get it into English this time. We think of the genius of the English language, what its *nature* is.

During this stage, we use all we know about the structure of the English language. During the composition of the literal version we followed the word order of the original language.

We now have to make it sound more like idiomatic English. We need to feel more confident, to get back into our own language. Leaving the word order of the original poem behind is often painful. Beginning translators, especially, resist it. They feel disloyal. But each language evolves in a different way.

After redoing the lines, thinking solely of the sentence and clause structures natural to English, we arrive at a new draft. We ignore the sentence structure of the original and try to move all sentences bodily into the genius of English. Along the way, we rephrase all the lines, so as to avoid being caught in the first phrases that have come to mind.

4

We translated the poem into English in the third stage. In the fourth stage we translate the poem into spoken American English. It is the achievement of the spoken quality that this stage aims at. Many translators stop before this stage.

We need the energy of spoken language as we try to keep a translation alive, just as we need the energy of written language. Every great poet mingles spoken language and written language in the most delicate way; the poem balances informal and formal tones. The aim is the living tone or "fragrance" that tells you a person alive now could have said the phrase. Robert Frost called this fragrance "sentence sound" and noted that it is not the rational mind that understands the distinction, but the ear and the ear's memory.

So during the fourth stage we begin to need the ear: We remember what people say to us. And we choose from the abundant possibilities the American language offers us until our ear feels better, until our ear remembers sentences like the ones we have come up with. Asking the ear about each phrase, "Have you ever heard this phrase spoken?" is the labor of this stage. The ear will reply with a few new phrases, and these act to shake up the translation once more and keep it from solidifying. The language becomes livelier, fresher, lighter.

5

In Bly's fifth stage we need the ear again—not the ear turned outward toward human speech but the ear turned inward toward the complicated feelings the poem is conveying. Each poem has a mood, a moment when the poet was able to catch a mood. Does our latest draft have the tone of the original?

To succeed in this stage it is important that the translator has written poetry himself; the translator needs the experience of writing from mood in order to judge accurately what the mood of a stranger's poem is. We need accurate judgment on mood now because in finding spoken phrases to replace the written we may have thrown the tone off. We may have the wrong tone of voice in the new phrases.

The problem of translating "upper language" or "noble language" into English is tremendous. The translator will end up with a translation that is "nobly dead" if, in the effort to rise to the upper or resonating level that he senses, he abandons our living language and resorts to old cloudlike phrases that are now only scenery. If he tries, from the best intentions, to retrieve and revive dusty clauses and high-flown diction and stuff them into the poem, the result is that the living language dies, both languages die, and the original poet seems ridiculous: the vividness is gone and the senses evaporate. The translation fails in tone. And that failure comes from pretending that the aristocratic stream of language is still alive in English. In English, we have to use the feeling stream only. We have no choice.

Changing the word order may change the mood, and for the sake of tone, we may have to replace a pronoun with its noun referent.

Summing up, in this stage we move to modify errors that may have come in with the emphasis on the spoken. Most of all we open ourselves for the first time to the mood of the poem. We try to be precise about what its mood is and so distinguish it from the mood of nearby poems. We try to capture the poem's balance of high and low, dark and light, ponderousness and light-heartedness.

6

In the sixth stage, we pay attention to sound. The question of tone has led to this. To find the poem's sound, there is only one thing to do: memorize the poem in its original language and speak it. We cannot translate well from a poem we haven't learned by heart: only by reciting it can we feel what sort of "oceanic rhythm" it has, as Bly calls it.

Here Bly distinguishes between two kinds of sound energies in a poem: one in the muscle system, which is a body motion, and one in the ear. The body motion alerts the mind and builds tension that is later released. The translator's job is to feel the body rhythm of each line. The second quality of sound—sound calling to sound—is related to internal rhyme. (If you memorize the poem in the original language and say it over many times, you will understand sound calling to sound without any other help.)

Keeping these two aspects of sound in mind, and saying the poem over in the original language many times, the translator may make changes for the sake of internal rhyme, or to shift the rhythm of a line or stanza, or to follow the original author's use of words from the same root.

One can never be sure, when helped by sound to a solution, whether the solution is reasonable or justifiable within the original author's area of meaning. The translator must decide what to emphasize and then set down a draft worked out after brooding over the original author's rhythm.

7

During Bly's seventh stage, we ask someone born into the language to go over our version. We ask him or her to find errors that have crept in.

For beginning translators, this stage is very painful. As beginners, we tend to give ourselves permission to veer away from the poem's images, pulled away by our own mental horses, and dismay sets in when we realize that some of our favorite solutions are simply wrong. None of us can learn a foreign language well enough to pick up everything.

During this stage we also have a second chance to ask about the implications of certain words that have begun to bother us. Sometimes knowing the roots of words in the original language helps us to choose a word in English.

If we have someone near at hand, then the labor of this stage can be done gradually, as the problems come up. If not, we should take on this stage by sheer will, and consider it as important as any of the earlier stages.

We have been slowly possessing the poem and making it ours — we have to do that to bring it alive — but we have to make sure that we have not kidnapped it instead.

8

Our last stage is making the final draft.

We read back over our earlier drafts — perhaps a half line was said better in one of them.

We have to make our final adjustments now.

During this stage we allow ourselves, at last, the pleasure of examining other people's translations of the poem. This is fun we can't deny ourselves after all our work, and we can sympathize with each translator.

After studying once more all our earlier drafts, and making our final sound and rhythm adjustments, and after taking in what we can from other people's translations and commentaries, we are ready to set down the final draft. Bly leaves us with a final point to ponder after all our work is done: "We know that we haven't captured the original: the best translation resembles a Persian rug seen from the back — the pattern is apparent, but not much more."

WILLIS BARNSTONE: "Letting in the Light: Translating Holy Texts" (2003)

> Translation is not mainly the work of preserving the hearth
> — a necessary task performed by scholarship —
> but of letting a fire burn in it.
> — critic Richard Eder (*New York Times*, February 22, 2000, p. 88)

Twenty years after Bly wrote his book, Willis Barnstone, one of the most recent translators of the Odes of Solomon into English, developed his own theory of translation in the book *The Poetics of Translation* (1995) and later reprised it in the introduction to his translation of the Odes in *The Gnostic Bible* (2003), "Letting in the Light: Translating Holy Texts." Not unexpectedly, Barnstone's theory concurs with the theories of both Rexroth and Bly.

For him the primary idea of translation is to make the aesthetic of the original shine in the translation. But he notes that for more than a century, translations of religious scripture have retained a formulaic, archaizing lexicon, and the aesthetic has disappeared in the transfer: "To maltreat Homer and Dante as sacred scripture like the Bible has been hurt would be literary heresy." Early in the twentieth century, the reigning poet and critic, T.S. Eliot, denounced Gilbert Murray's wooden versions of the Greek classics, but no similar regal figure has yet demanded new and vibrant versions of sacred scripture.

Religious scholars have the ancient tongues to bring meaning to obscure alphabets. That is their enormous virtue and power. And scholarly translation of religious scripture in facing-page editions are laudable tools for reading and understanding a foreign-language page. And word-for-word versions are a good initial step to converting a foreign-language page. But no one should imagine that they capture or reproduce the poetry of the original. Barnstone strongly states his observation:

> In rendering ancient languages into English, each age has its own speech and demand for a natural reading experience. Most important, if the original is worth transferring to English, it must be rich in sound and sense and sovereign in art. If scripture or myth, it has survived because of its breath and its style. Those prophets who spoke magical words were not literary clods. Not if they were to be heard. To make a work heard again, the translator must re-create that cunning of art. Then a text can move pleasantly from foreign obscurity into the light of our own familiar tongue.

Barnstone recognizes that there is no single secret of literary translation, and the ways of translation have diverse linguistic and aesthetic variables, but there is a best way:

> If the scholar and writer artist are one person, it is ideal. However, even the most erudite non-artist scholar, apart form creating a gloss, can only do harm to the aesthetic of the original. Likewise, if the writer artist disdains knowledge of the source text, the result may be lovely but will not go beyond imitation. A frequent solution is to put scholars and writers together. . . . Commonly an informant and a writer collaborate intelligently as one voice.

Pragmatically, he knows there must be a meeting between the original creator and the writer who re-creates. When Robert Fitzgerald asked the older poet Ezra Pound how to render Homer into English, Pound said simply, "Let Homer speak." This is the kind of meeting Barnstone attempted with his translation of what he calls the "delicious songs of Solomon from the Syriac."

The Project of Translating the Odes of Solomon

UNLIKE MOST POEMS, the Odes are true spiritual expressions of feeling in response to God's Light. But they are not simply the expressions of the idiosyncracies of a single peculiar person, the descendant of a particular family or tribe, with particular inherent cultural and social conflicts and inner traumas. There are cultural and social and inner traumas and conflicts expressed in the Odes, but they are representative expressions of a member of the universal society and community of the spiritually reborn — the enlightened congregation of the new and, at the time, unpopular messianic Community of individuals gathered under God for the purpose of exemplifying, teaching, maintaining, and promoting the spiritual restoration of the world.

This is the reason that the expressions of the Odes are at once personal and universal. They are expressions of the enlightened human spirit under the conditions of a specific time, but they are expressions that can be understood and sympathized with for all time. Like the impersonal experiments of modern physical science, the personal experiences that the Odes express can be and have been reproduced. That is the nature of spiritual knowledge. And the Odes are expressions of such a knowledge. As a translator, my purpose has been less to translate the sound of the Odes and more to bring out the sense — the feeling, the knowledge, the teaching, and the communal understanding and assumptions — that the Odes express. They are expressions of one who followed The Way.

There are a few special difficulties that come with the attempt to translate the Odes into English. First is the general tendency among English-speaking translators, and especially among scholars, to translate all ancient spiritual literature into an imitation of the beautiful, but now somewhat bombastic, King James English. All English translations of the Odes suffer from this tendency. It is almost inescapable. To begin with, the language of the Odes is by its nature "biblical," and the Protestant Reformation has made biblical language King Jamesian. Second, all translations work off of the first English translation of the Odes made by James Rendel Harris, the discoverer of the Odes, who did his work of translation one hundred years ago. Harris's translation is rhythmic and feeling and musical, but metaphysically often rather flat and incoherent. Whatever lines of the Odes that more recent translators have renovated or changed still live in the old neighborhood of Harris's lines. At times this is true of my own translation as well. Third, all translators mirror themselves in the poems they translate, whether they understand those poems or not. This is also true of myself as a translator. And I believe that I can say (I hope without seeming arrogant) that the difference between me and other translators is that I recognize what the author of the Odes was talking about from my own firsthand experience and not only, like the others, by comparing the ideas and language of the Odes with other scriptural texts.

Even though I was for the most part ignorant of the ancient language of the Odes when I began this project, I was able to accomplish my work of translation, and could presume to possess some understanding of these poems, because of my sympathies. I was able to recognize in the words of the Odes, even in the jumbled translations that now exist, that the process of spiritual regeneration was being depicted in them. I recognized in the Odes the same knowledge and the same liturgical practice and the same messianic spiritual force being received and attuned to. Such spiritual recognition and knowledge is certainly not the possession of scholars who have attempted to translate the Odes for us in our time, at least not entirely, just as their knowledge and recognitions are not entirely mine. But I have, to the best of my ability, made the fruits of their work mine, just as I hope they will someday make the fruits of my work their own, so that together we may approach the study of the origin and purpose of the Odes.

I, within the spiritual Community of which I am a part, have been doing for decades, liturgically, what the author of the Odes and his spiritual Community were doing 2000 years ago — and what few others are doing, and few others have done, over the past

2000 years. And those few who have done something similar over the last two millennia were mystic practitioners of "esoteric arts" who were pledged not to divulge their secret practices. But the time has now come in our age — the Second Advent Age, the age of the Second Coming — to make the esoteric *exoteric*, so that all individuals and peoples of the world may know what in the Odes is called "Goodness" and so seek to be redeemed.

And that is why I have undertaken this work of translation. The Odes, as ancient texts, are images and mirrors of the early messianic Communities that grew up under Jesus and his direct followers. But those Communities lasted for only a few generations. The Odes assume practices and doctrines which, since that time, have been forgotten. These ancient practices and doctrines have now been renewed, restored, and regenerated in a new spiritual Community that has inherited them along with the tradition of this ancient Community. This new Community has built an educational institution to teach and preserve them and amend them for our times. But before the "new" news can be understood as it has been revealed, the "old" news needs to be understood truly. It needs to be purified of the modifications, deletions, suppositions, mistakes, intellectual pilings, and outright lies that surround and have grown into the fabric of the original and beautiful and once pristine teachings. My attempt to translate the Odes is part of this purification process. I hope others after me will be able to do better for their times. And I hope too that a real poet who has the same sensibility and understandings as I have may someday arise and make these Odes into the modern poems that they deserve to be.

*

For myself, I cannot claim to be a poet. And I did not know a word of Coptic or Syriac when I undertook the project of attempting to translate the Odes of Solomon into coherent American English. The Odes, like all poems, employ the beauties and intricacies of language to express ideas and feelings. And the sounds of the poems in Syriac are, for the most part, still unfamiliar to me. But their significant use of words, their etymological roots and multiple meanings in particular passages, has been pointed out by scholars, and I have made use of their points in the making of my translations.

I began my own translation with the sonorous 1920 translation of James Rendel Harris, revised and modernized by purifying it of the sovereign plurals and archaisms of the King James English which it imitated. In the first zeal of translation of a book of poems nearly two thousand years old, a book not copied for 500 years, Harris missed letters and markings in manuscripts whose washed out pages have since been magnified and gone over more carefully by scholars in the 100 years after him. Even so, the poems are written on manuscripts that are now so timeworn and mutilated and badly copied that three generations of scholars cannot at all times agree on what words are written there. My own scholarship is incomplete and the number of my references rather meager.[1] So to make this translation, I have had to count on my many hours of concentrated study and consideration over a period of two years and my own spiritual knowledge and experience.

The contemporary American poet Robert Bly, in his 1986 essay *The Eight Stages of Translation*, attempted to describe what it is like to translate a poem, looking primarily at the difficulties. To explain what I have attempted to do in my translation, I will make direct reference to the eight ideal stages of translation which he identified and explained:[2]

---

[1] Of the references I have kept at hand I should mention the following:
A Concise Coptic-English Lexicon, Second Edition, by Richard Smith (Society of Biblical Literature, 2000)
A Coptic Dictionary Compiled by W. E. Crum (Oxford at Clarendon press, 1939)
A Compendious Grammar of the Egyptian Language by Rev. Henry Tattam (John and Arthur Arch, 1830)
A Compendious Syriac Grammar by Theodor Nöldeke (Wipf and Stock Publishers, 2003; previously published by Williams & Nargate, 1904)
A Compendious Syriac Dictionary edited by J. Payne Smith (Wipf and Stock Publishers, 1999; previously published by Oxford University Press, 1902)
Odes of Solomon, A Commentary by Michael Lattke, Marianne Ehrhardt, translator (Fortress Press, 2009)
The Odes of Solomon, The Syriac Texts edited with translation and notes by James Hamilton Charlesworth (Scholars Press, 1977)
Papyri and Lleather Manuscripts of the Odes of Solomon edited by J. H. Charlesworth (International Center for the Study of Ancient Near Eastern Civilization and Christian Origins, Duke University, 1981)
Syriac Dictionary Online Translation LEXILOGOS (www.lexilogos.com/english/syriac_dictionary.htm)
[2] For a summary of Bly's eight stages, see the addendum,"Three Poets on Translating Poetry."

1: Setting down a literal version of the poem

Dr. James. H. Charlesworth and Dr. Michael Lattke have provided careful literal translations of the Odes. My own translation follows the Syriac text, and for Ode 1, the Coptic text, as well as the literal translation of the Odes that has been so carefully completed and so thoroughly noted by Dr. Charlesworth (1973, 1978). When I later discovered Dr. Lattke's book, I made extensive corrections using his copious discussions of especially complex phrases. Lattke provided hundreds of pages of line-by-line discussion on the individual words of the Odes in their contexts. And the English concordance that he appended to his translation of the Odes has provided me with indispensable pointers to every single word used in the Odes. And while I have not always agreed with the interpretation he has argued for, or his word choices when other meanings of the Syriac words proved more fruitful, his discussion of specific words and phrases have always added to my understanding.

2: Finding out what the poem means

To find the meaning of the Odes was another matter. Still the notes of Dr. Charlesworth and Dr. Lattke did much to clarify the possible meanings of important single words and phrases and the tenses and moods of verbs. And I can say that I had little "resistance," to use Bly's term, to what the poet was saying. Nearly all the poet's feelings and concepts are "within my world." There are exceptions of course. And there are cultural references that I had to struggle with and guess at — references which no scholar or historian has yet addressed suitably or directly. But to figure out what each word was doing in the Odes, in order to make each Ode clear, I have searched for and adopted what I believe are appropriate solutions.

Charlesworth in his notes comments several times that other translators have failed to translate singular nouns as singular and have instead translated them as plurals. In all these cases the nouns apply to a collective body made up of individuals gathered together in spirit. My thought is that the collective body, the Community that is referred to, is given importance or recognition in this way, a way that is perhaps not generally comprehended by most moderns. The Community or Congregation that is referred to has a life of its own, as if it were an organism in itself made up of individual members, an organism that produces its own metanoia.

Charlesworth and Lattke have presented many alternate meanings to phrases and words in the Odes. In my own translation I have incorporated, when it seemed appropriate, these alternative phrases by doubling them up in the translation when the original Syriac wordplay would otherwise be untranslatable or invisible or impossible to catch or interpret in English. There are numerous instances of double meanings. Rather than choose only one or the other of the possible meanings for my translation, wherever such words appear and I am able to recognize them, I have doubled up the phrasing rather than choosing only one meaning or the other. In this way, it seems to me, the sense is enriched. Translating in this fashion has put more words in some of the phrases than there are in the original but brings through to a modern reader the meaning and sense of these phrases with a clarity more like what the original phrases must have had 2000 years ago.

And there are some specific references that have, I think, been misunderstood or left ambiguous by other translators. Two of the major sources of misunderstanding are the use of the words *Lord* and *Son of Man* in the Odes. The references made in the Odes to the word *Lord* in the Odes sometimes refers to the Lord Messiah and sometimes to the Lord God. When the reference seems unclear, I have used syntax to indicate the referent or else have added the word "God" or "Most High" or "Anointed." Many translators have assumed that the "Son of God" mentioned in the poems is always the Messiah, Christ Jesus, speaking at various points throughout the Odes. This is a presumption imposed upon the Odes and the poet of the Odes, and is not always the case. Much of the time the "Son of God" is the poet himself, who has been transformed and become a Child of God.

For the most part, in the hands of every previous translator, each poem has been made into an incoherent and disjointed mass of splendid words and images. In my translation, I have attempted to remedy this condition by discovering and displaying the singular coherent feeling that each poem presents. For they are poems after all, and not theological or theosophical ciphers.

3: Redoing the literal version to get it into natural English and recover the meaning we have just found

I have referred back to the notes of both Charlesworth and Lattke continually through the translation process to see where the literal translations did not allow the meaning to come through clearly while I was, at the same time, trying to move the sense of verses and sentences into natural American English. Where I found the literal version of a phrase or verse set out by scholars to be inadequate or senseless, I have gone through painstaking work to reconstruct the phrasings by laying out all the possible senses I could see for each word in each phrase before coming up with my solution.

4: Translating the poem into spoken American English to get the energy of the spoken language

I have treated the half-lines of each verse as rhythmic units, and I have tried in my translation to make each of these units into phrases that could easily and comfortably be spoken out loud, phrases that as spoken words convey the feeling or thought that I believe the poet of the Odes intended to convey.

5: Translating the tone and mood of the poem

There are two tenses in Syriac: perfect and imperfect, which express past and future. The present is expressed by using the active participle with personal pronouns (as in *I am going*). In English, the perfect is expressed by the use of auxiliary verbs (*had* and *has* or *have*). In the Odes, the distinction between present perfect (for example, *has* or *have gone*) and past perfect (for example, *had gone*) must be drawn from the context in which the verb occurs. I have at times read the context differently than previous translators, and so at times I have translated verbs in the present perfect where others have translated them as past perfect.

Not being knowledgeable in all the subtleties of the conjugations of verbs in Syriac, despite my attempts to be, I have followed the lead of either Charlesworth or Lattke. But when the perfect sense of verbs seemed to me to indicate a continued sense (as in the phrase *have done*) rather than a completed sense (*did*), I have followed the sense of the images being created in the poem to make my translation. To catch the mood and what I believe must have been the original tone of each poem, in order to make them again in living English, I have counted more on my own spiritual and liturgical experience than my experience in writing poems. And I hope that my spiritual experience suffices and makes up for my lack of experience at writing poems. For clarity, I have sometimes replaced pronouns with their noun referent and doubled up the meanings of particularly potent word images.

6: Paying attention to sound

My general ignorance of the sound of spoken Syriac has not permitted me to pay much attention to the sound of the original poems. Perhaps time and study will permit me, or better, some future poet, to attempt to reproduce the rhythm and original sounds of the poems.

I have, however, attempted to keep some of the repetitive sounds I could recognize. For one example, the Syriac phrase that indicates spiritual immortality, immortal life, or undying life, is in my translation translated as "The Life That Does Not Die" in order to keep the Syriac phrasing and in order to avoid the abstract sound of a phrase like "immortal life" and to keep the spiritual drama at the forefront. For another example, in the Odes there is an abundant use of the conjunctions *and* and *and so* and of the negatives *no*, *not*, and *nor*. I have tried to keep both these terms in my translation, both to follow the Syriac constructions and to keep the repetitive sounds going. Likewise, instead of using the word *without*, whenever it was possible to do so I have used *with no* or some other such phrase to keep the negative sound in the sentence.

7: Finding a native speaker who can go over our version and find the errors that may have crept in

There are no native speakers of ancient Syriac, and I have not been able to ask a trained Syriac scholar to go over my version of the poems to find errors that may have crept in. It is my hope that this part of the translation process will occur after publication of the present translation, if it attracts review and criticism, and that I will be able to provide improvements for a future amended edition.

8: Making the final draft

To come up with final drafts, I have gone over problematic phrases and ideas again and again as carefully and as thoroughly as I was able. Where other translators have simply made verses into a series of independent clauses, I have used punctuation abundantly in my translation in order to make connections between verses and to subordinate phrases and thoughts to indicate the overall coherence of each poem. And where a speaker in the poem is not the poet himself, I have enclosed their words in quotation marks. Odes 8-10, I believe, are intended to be the words of the Messiah, the Anointed One, as is Ode 42. The Anointed One is also quoted within Ode 31. The Virgin Goodness is quoted within Ode 33. And within Ode 11, the poet quotes himself as he was speaking with the Lord God in a vision. Quotation marks do not appear in the original manuscripts.

In the Syriac manuscripts, verses and their component half-lines are indicated by markings. In my translation, individual verses are indicated by indenting. Half-lines are also indicated, wherever possible, by punctuation. I have tended to over-punctuate the verses in my translation in order to indicate the half-lines that make them up, except where punctuation would interfere with the sense, or where the half-lines are a subject and its predicate, or where the half-lines are obviously in parallel construction. Some verses in the poems are a single line. Most are composed of two half-lines, and others of three or more. To further reflect the coherence of the sequence of utterances in each poem, I have marked what seems to me pauses or changes in speech or thought with spacing to separate each separate utterance, thereby forming something like verse paragraphs. These are my own constructions and are not indicated in the original text.

* *

All in all, I cannot say that I have made the Odes sing. But I can say that I have made them speak, and perhaps more clearly and coherently than any other translation to date has done.

About the Author

ROBERT PETROVICH is a spiritual educator, counselor and canon of the International Community of Christ, and a senior member of Cosolargy International. For over twenty years he has held a position on the faculty of The Academy for Advancement in the Religious Arts, Sciences and Technologies of Cosolargy®.

To order additional copies of this book, or to schedule a talk, presentation, or workshop, contact Robert Petrovich directly by phone (775-786-7431, ext. 105) or email (robert@cosolargy.org).

For information on Cosolargy International, visit www.cosolargy.org.

www.ingramcontent.com/pod-product-compliance
Lightning Source LLC
Chambersburg PA
CBHW021139080526
44588CB00008B/136